MASSAGE
—FOR—
COMMON
AILMENTS

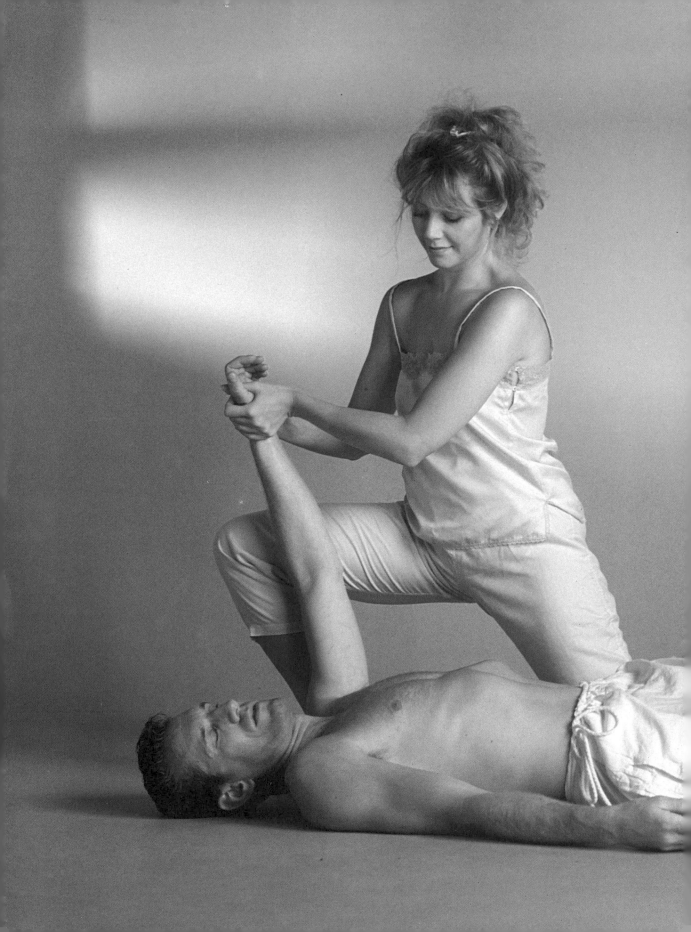

MASSAGE
—FOR—
COMMON
AILMENTS

Sara Thomas

Photography by Fausto Dorelli

SIDGWICK & JACKSON
LONDON

A GAIA ORIGINAL

Written by Sara Thomas

with Jane Downer and Chris Jarmey
of the Shiatsu School of Natural Therapy, London

Photography	Fausto Dorelli
Editorial	Joanna Godfrey Wood Susan McKeever
Design	Lynn Hector
Illustration	Sheilagh Noble
Production	Susan Walby
Direction	Lucy Lidell Patrick Nugent Casey Horton

COLLINS PUBLISHERS AUSTRALIA

First published in Australasia in 1989 by William Collins
Pty Ltd.
55 Clarence Street, Sydney NSW 2000

National Library of Australia
Cataloguing-in-Publication data:

Thomas, Sara.

Massage for common ailments.

ISBN 0 7322 2489 6.

1. Massage – Handbooks, manuals, etc. I. Title.
615.8'22

Typeset in Gill by Marlin Graphics Ltd, Kent, England
Reproduction by F.E. Burman Ltd, London
Printed and bound in Spain by
Artes Graficas Toledo SA
D.L.TO.: 2385/1988

About this book

Two separate, but overlapping, therapies are introduced in Massage for Common Ailments – massage and Shiatsu. All the sequences for treating ailments are derived from massage unless the heading states Shiatsu. You can use them individually or together to help the healing process.

Before you start treating an ailment, take time to study Basic Strokes (see pp.22-7) and When Massage Should Not Be Used (see p.93). The main part of the book, Common Ailments (pp.28-89), is divided into separate sections that deal with different parts of the body, starting with the head and working down to the feet. The charts on pp. 30-1 show you where in the body the various ailments occur.

Note Always consult a doctor if you are in doubt about a medical condition, and observe the cautions given in the book.

The use of the hands
as a means to convey friendship
to comfort and heal the sick
to express love and tenderness
to quiet and titillate the child
is as old as life

Bernard Gunter

Touch affects the body's vital forces

Jerome Liss

To permit simple contact is to permit,
and necessarily to experience,
the natural reinforcement
that the living has for the living.

Charles Brooks

CONTENTS

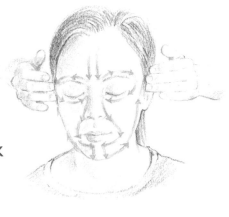

INTRODUCTION

Throughout history we have used our hands to impart comfort and healing to one another. Touching is contact, warmth, reassurance that we are not alone, affirmation of our sense of being and self-worth. It is a simple way of communicating, something we all do naturally. And with a little willingness and commitment we can turn this natural talent into a creative healing skill, by learning the basic strokes and techniques of massage and widening our vocabulary in the language of touch.

Our sense of touch is registered by our skin – our largest and most sensitive organ. In the developing embryo, the skin arises from the same cell layer as the nervous system and can thus be seen as the external portion of the nervous system – able to receive and register a vast quantity of varied signals, and to make a wide range of responses to them. Also, touch is the first sense to become functional in the embryo.

The value of massage

The intent that goes with touch makes all the difference to its effect. When we lay our hands on another with compassion and good-will many subtle changes take place. Gentle holding and stroking, touching given with tenderness and care, cause transformations both physically and psychologically.

In the 1920s in Philadelphia the anatomist Frederick Hammett and other American researchers in the 1950s and 60s conducted experiments with groups of rats to investigate the effects of touch. Some were consistently handled and stroked and others were not. The rats that were regularly touched showed faster growth rates, better immunity to disease and higher fertility and were less subject to stress than those that were not. It is well known, too, that for infants, fondling and tender touch that go beyond the basic needs for food and cleanliness are vital for life. In America, between 1910 and 1935, studies of babies in institutions were conducted by Drs. Chapin and Knox and J. Brennemann. They found that many babies died in infancy and others showed clear signs of disturbance and poor physical and emotional development as a result of too little tactile stimulation.

Physiologically, caring touch and massage help the flow of blood and lymph in our bodies. Touch can also decrease our blood pressure and heart rate, soothe our nerves and decrease tension, producing relaxation and a state of well-being. It has been suggested that massage may aid the production of endorphins

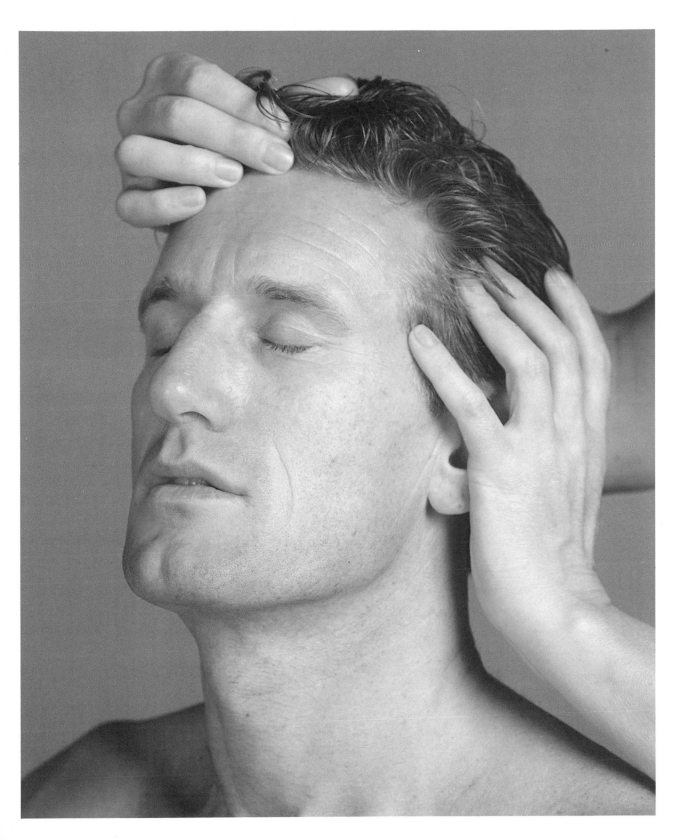

(meaning "morphine within"), the brain chemicals that function as natural pain-killers. One of these, enkephalin, has the ability to reduce pain and produces a state of mind akin to euphoria.

The experience of being nourished and cared for and allowing ourselves to receive healing touch affirms our self-esteem, creates trust and openness and can sometimes facilitate the release of blocked emotions as tense muscles relax. Touch can make us feel valued, peaceful and more aware of our whole body and being.

It is not only receiving touch that is beneficial, however. Giving massage is also highly rewarding. There is pleasure in the physical contact and in feeling the contours and undulations of the body as you begin to develop a sense of the muscles, bones and other tissues. There is enjoyment in knowing the body, in being alive to its different tensions and energies, and in realizing that you can care for and help another. There is also satisfaction in experiencing the results of your massage as you feel muscles relaxing and realize that your concern and your touch can help to stimulate the receiver's own healing process. Often the interaction between the giver and receiver induces a similar state in both – a state that is very similar to meditation.

The Chakras

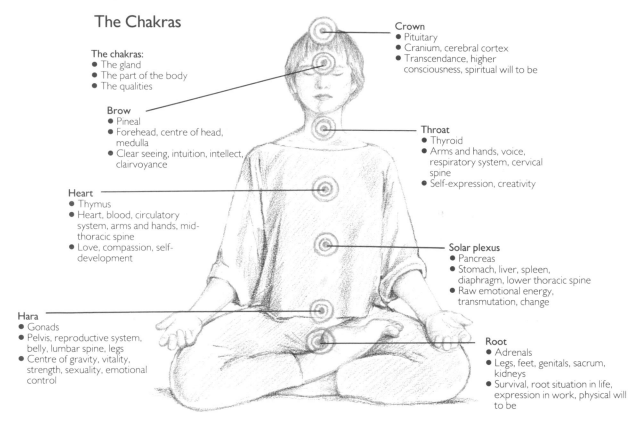

The chakras:
- The gland
- The part of the body
- The qualities

Crown
- Pituitary
- Cranium, cerebral cortex
- Transcendance, higher consciousness, spiritual will to be

Brow
- Pineal
- Forehead, centre of head, medulla
- Clear seeing, intuition, intellect, clairvoyance

Throat
- Thyroid
- Arms and hands, voice, respiratory system, cervical spine
- Self-expression, creativity

Heart
- Thymus
- Heart, blood, circulatory system, arms and hands, mid-thoracic spine
- Love, compassion, self-development

Solar plexus
- Pancreas
- Stomach, liver, spleen, diaphragm, lower thoracic spine
- Raw emotional energy, transmutation, change

Hara
- Gonads
- Pelvis, reproductive system, belly, lumbar spine, legs
- Centre of gravity, vitality, strength, sexuality, emotional control

Root
- Adrenals
- Legs, feet, genitals, sacrum, kidneys
- Survival, root situation in life, expression in work, physical will to be

Balancing the flow of vital energy

Wholeness goes beyond the body, mind and emotions. In wholeness is health, and in any kind of healing touch technique you are treating more than just the physical body; you are also affecting a person's "subtle" body and restoring balance to the flow of energy. This subtle body includes the energy field or "aura", in and around the body, and the major centres of subtle energy or vitality known as the *chakras*. The aura is composed of inter-penetrating fields of subtle or vital energy that emanates from the body, out beyond the periphery of the skin, and is constantly in motion. Within the aura and along the midline of the body are the seven main *chakras*, whose function is to relay vital energy between the physical body and the subtle body. The word *chakra* is a Sanskrit word meaning wheel, which indicates the circling movement of energy in these centres. Five are situated on the spine and two in the head. They relate to different parts of the body – to glands, organs, and nerve plexii, and also to areas of our psychological and spiritual development. With practice you can learn to sense the energies of the aura and *chakras* with your hands.

Using Shiatsu as a healing tool

In this book, we have chosen to teach not only massage but also Shiatsu to give you a wider range of effective techniques for the relief of everyday health problems.

Shiatsu has its origins in Oriental medicine. The word literally means finger or thumb pressure, although other parts of the hand and body are also used. In Japan Shiatsu has traditionally been practiced as a simple remedy to promote health, alleviate pain and prevent sickness. Its techniques are based on the understanding that the body functions as a whole, linked by vital energy, or *ki*, which flows along channels, or meridians, which interlace as a network throughout the body, mostly on the skin's surface. Discomfort, pain, stress and illness are caused by *ki* energy stagnating and "blocking" the meridians, making the internal organs either deficient in or overloaded by energy. By holding and applying pressure to points, or *tsubos*, on the meridians, you can stimulate the *ki* energy, helping it to rebalance itself. This affects the physical body and can help to relieve pain and alleviate the causes and symptoms of illness.

Shiatsu should not be painful. Although some *tsubos* and meridians may be tender, pressure can be applied gently and slowly, so that it always feels comfortable. Shiatsu is a form of communication, and its effectiveness is dependent on a willingness to be open and receptive to your partner.

Shiatsu Meridians

Key to the meridians

Bl	Bladder	Ht	Heart	TH	Triple heater
Ki	Kidney	Lu	Lungs	HP	Heart protector
Liv	Liver	GB	Gall bladder	GV	Governing vessel
St	Stomach	SI	Small intestines	CV	Conception vessel.
Sp	Spleen	LI	Large intestines		

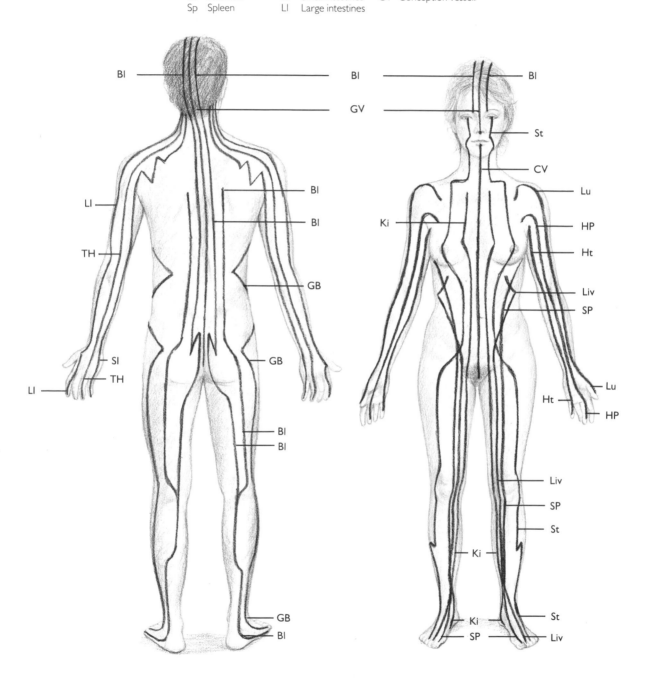

N.B. All the meridians are mirrored on the other side of the body.

Preventing and treating ill health with massage

When you already have the gift of health you need to maintain it. Touch does not just have to be used as a way of healing and hastening recovery – it can also be a way of preventing sickness. In today's "civilized" cultures it is only too easy to get caught up in striving, accomplishing, and conforming to society's mores. In the process you can become overly head-orientated and out of touch with your body. This also means being out of touch with reality, however, for it is through your body that you receive sensory messages that let you know what you need, what you are feeling emotionally, and what is happening around you in the immediate environment. This is all vital information for self-regulation, in the sense of giving your body what is best for health and balance. In order to be truly healthy you need to stop thinking that ideas and concepts are the only reality and wake up to the information that your whole body can give you. As Fritz Perls, the founder of Gestalt therapy, said "lose your head and come to your senses".

Massage is a way of getting back in touch with your body and finding trust in what it has to say. When you become more aware of yourself as a whole being, physical, mental, emotional and spiritual, you can start to respond more to fulfilling your real needs. Eating a healthy and balanced diet, exercising daily and breathing more freely can all be done with a sense of pleasure and rightness rather than as chores or acts of grim will-power.

Nevertheless, everyone gets sick from time to time, and illness is often a manifestation of the body's attempt to heal itself and to eliminate toxins and clear the system. This book is about how to use touch to help the body's natural healing process when you or your family or friends do succumb to any of the common ailments. It is not about miracle cures, but about giving warmth and support to another by a variety of caring touch techniques, which can help to speed recovery. As many illnesses result from stress and strain in daily life, the touch therapies are particularly effective, for they calm and soothe tension and bring balance to your being. Both massage and Shiatsu work with and for the body's healing energies; in contrast to states of stress and effort they create the conditions for healing to take place. As well as learning how to do a whole body massage, which you can use when an ailment is more general and affects the whole body – such as insomnia or fatigue – you will also learn strokes and techniques to aid more specific conditions, such as headaches, backaches, constipation and cramp. Use the book wisely. Don't try to take over a doctor's role – give where you can and seek medical advice where you can't. Your hands have healing in them. Use them.

BEGINNING

In order to help another by our touch we need to be caring, willing to give some time and to focus our attention fully on our partner. Just ten minutes of touch given by someone who is really present and caring can be far more beneficial than an hour of mechanical massage by someone whose mind is absent or distracted. So it is important to prepare yourself before beginning by centring yourself (see p.19). With a little practice you will become familiar enough with this centred state to be able to let go of your busy mind and come into the here and now at short notice. By staying centred you are able to tune in more fully to the areas of your partner's body that need a special touch or movement.

While giving massage and Shiatsu, "grounding" is also very important. This means being fully aware of your own body and its movements and position and letting these movements emanate from your pelvis and *hara* (see p.19), not just from your shoulders and arms. When you use your *hara* you use your relationship with the ground to get in touch with your strength. You save yourself from fatigue as strength comes from your whole body and all your movements are more gracefully controlled and more effective.

When doing massage or Shiatsu to alleviate common ailments you may find you have to improvise in situations or places that are not ideal. But even in unconducive environments, healing touch can bring welcome relief. However, if you have planned a massage in advance you will be able to set the scene and create an environment that is as warm and nurturing as possible. Without too much difficulty you can turn a room into a cosy space with everything you need at hand.

Once your environment is prepared there are a few guidelines for both giver and receiver to remember. When giving either massage or Shiatsu you should wear loose light clothing, as the room will be warm and your clothes should allow freedom of movement. You need to remove your watch, any bracelets and rings and your fingernails should be short to avoid scratching and you should wash your hands thoroughly. Throughout the treatment you need to remain receptive to what you are feeling with your hands. Avoid chatting but by all means communicate when necessary about pressure and discomfort. Shiatsu is done with the receiver fully clothed, but for massage the receiver should remove whatever clothes are necessary, plus watches and jewellery, and once lying down should relax and yield to gravity. The role of the receiver is not entirely passive. He or she needs to keep aware of the giver's touch and of the sensations being experienced.

Creating the environment

When making a conducive environment in which to do either massage or Shiatsu there are several elements to consider. First, the room needs to be warm, as we tense up when chilled. For oil massage this is especially important, so have an extra heater on hand. A selection of small towels and pillows is also useful if you need to pad under any area of your partner's body, such as the ankles, belly or upper chest, when he or she is face down, or the knees when face up. Shiatsu is always done on the floor – on a pad or futon covered with a sheet or towel. This is fine for massage too, but if you are uncomfortable working on the floor, it is worth investing in a massage table. Avoid ordinary beds as they are usually too soft and the wrong height. However, for both massage and Shiatsu, many of the strokes and techniques can be given while the receiver sits in a chair. Lighting should be very gentle as our eyes cannot fully relax in glaring light. Some people like to work to a background of peaceful and unobtrusive music, others prefer quietness. In any case make sure you won't be disturbed. Finally, have a large warm towel ready to place gently over your partner's body at the end of massage. For Shiatsu, use a blanket and allow your partner to relax for several minutes.

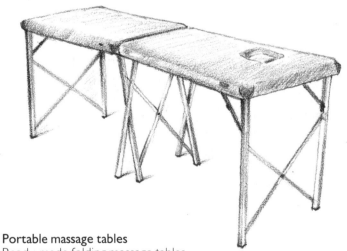

Portable massage tables
Ready-made folding massage tables are useful for those who find working on the floor difficult. Those with cross-over central legs are the most secure. Some tables, like the one shown here, also have face holes for people whose necks are too stiff to turn easily when lying on their fronts. The table should be about the same height as your palm if held parallel to the floor when your arm is hanging at your side.

Improvising with a chair
If your partner cannot get down on to the floor or up on to a table, you can use an ordinary chair. Your partner can either sit normally, so that you can work on neck, head, shoulders, hands, knees and feet. Or he or she can sit astride, as shown, resting head and arms on the back. Like this you can treat back, shoulders and neck very effectively.

Centring and the *hara*

In both massage and Shiatsu centring and grounding, or being focused and aware in the present, are of great importance. For it is by being wholly in the here and now that you can be of greatest help to your partner when you attempt to heal or help through touch. The *hara* (see also p.12) is situated in the belly, an inch or so below the navel, and is the centre of strength and vitality as well as the centre of gravity in the body. It links also with your legs and your connection to the ground, which gives you stability, hence the importance of using this centre for massage, and of letting the body move from here as you work. By directing your energy from this area your whole body becomes involved in the movements and you avoid fatigue and work more effectively. The meditation and exercise that follow will help you to centre yourself in your *hara*. If you have the chance, you should use it before any massage.

Centring and grounding meditation
Kneel or sit comfortably. Close your eyes and go inside yourself. Become aware of your legs, your feet and your buttocks, and where they make contact with the surface beneath. Try to feel your legs and pelvis as a firm base for your body, and then feel your spine rising gently up from it. Become aware of your trunk, shoulders, arms and hands and relax any tensions you might find. Then move slowly to your neck and head, letting go of any tightness around your eyes or in your jaw. Now let your attention turn to your breath and watch it coming in and out, like the waves on a beach. As you breathe in, let the breath sink more deeply into your *hara* and imagine it as light or energy filling your belly. Then, as you exhale, imagine the energy travelling down your arms and out through your hands. Notice the feeling in your hands as you do this.

After a few minutes place your hands lightly on your hips and begin to rotate your whole body slowly from the pelvis. Be aware of your legs and pelvis as a strong foundation and let your back and spine remain straight but not rigid. Having circled in one direction for a while, change and go the other way. Finally, rest and open your eyes.

Beginning an oil massage

You can use a variety of oils for massaging and will need to experiment to find out what suits you best. Suitable oils range from vegetable oils, such as sunflower, safflower or almond oil, to baby oils, which are mineral-based, or ready-mixed massage oils. If you enjoy scents and wish to enhance the effects of your massage with the therapeutic benefits of aromatherapy essences, you can add drops of these to a base of vegetable oil (see p.21).

At the start of a massage, before applying oils, you can make an initial acquaintance with your partner's body by means of a gentle touch, as shown below. You should apply oil only to the area that is to be worked on, rather than oiling the whole body at once. Oiling is done with long, smooth gliding strokes (see p.23), which spread a thin film of oil over the skin and also serve to warm and energize it. Don't overdo the amount of oil, but be more generous with areas such as hairy chests.

Throughout a massage, the way in which you make and break contact is extremely important, for if you suddenly "dive" on to the body it can be a shock to the receiver, and likewise, if you leap rapidly away with your hands, the harmony can be broken. It is not necessary to maintain a constant contact during a massage, however. Gentle breaks in touch, made with sensitivity, are like spaces of quietness within a passage of music.

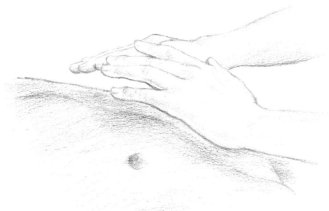

Applying oils
When you are ready to apply the oil (see below), hold your hands well away from your partner's body to avoid drips and pour a small amount of oil into one palm. Then rub your palms together, warming and spreading the oil, before bringing your hands gently to the body to start the oiling strokes.

Making contact
Centre yourself and allow your hands to float slowly down to a part of your partner's body, such as the head or back, and then rest lightly there for a few moments (see above). When you feel you have established the initial contact, lift your hands very gently away in order to begin oiling.

Aromatherapy essences

These essences (also known as essential oils) are obtained from the distillation of plants, flowers and herbs that have different therapeutic effects on the body. They also add the dimension of fragrant variety to enhance your massage and make it more healing and pleasurable. These essences have many different properties, ranging from effects on mood (i.e. antidepressant) to physical effects, such as anti-inflammatory and antibacterial. As they are very concentrated, aromatherapy essences always need to be diluted in a carrier oil before being applied to the skin, where they are absorbed quite quickly and enter the bloodstream. The best carrier oils are those of vegetable origin, such as soya, almond, or avocado. It is best to blend fairly small amounts of oil and essences as vegetable oil oxidizes and smells somewhat rancid after a while. A teaspoon of wheatgerm oil in a mix acts as an antioxidant. In the book, various essences are mentioned and suggested for different ailments.

Useful amounts:
*For full body: 5 drops of essence in 2 eggcupsful of carrier oil.
For body parts: 2-3 drops of essence in 1 eggcupful of carrier oil.
For small, localized areas: 1 drop of essence in one teaspoonful of carrier oil.*

Some aromatherapy essences

BERGAMOT	Antiseptic, antidepressant – uplifting and refreshing	Helps: depression, bronchitis, sore throat, digestive problems	LAVENDER	Antidepressant, antiseptic, sedative – refreshing and relaxing	Helps: depression, insomnia, flatulence, indigestion, asthma, bronchitis, menstrual pains, skin problems
CAMOMILE	Sedative – calming, refreshing and relaxing	Helps: aching muscles, headaches, menstrual pains, inflammations, stress, digestive problems	MARJORAM	Sedative, antiseptic – warming and strengthening	Helps: muscular pains, digestive problems, painful joints, sinus congestion
CARDAMOM	Antiseptic, tonic – refreshing	Helps: ease wind and digestive problems, painful joints, nausea, headaches, general debility	MELISSA	Antidepressant – uplifting and refreshing	Helps: headaches, migraine, menstrual pains, lowers high blood pressure
EUCALYPTUS	Antiseptic – head-clearing, stimulating	Helps: coughs, colds, bronchitis, aching muscles	ROSEMARY	Antiseptic – refreshing and stimulating	Helps: headaches, migraine, colds, bronchitis, muscular pains
FENNEL	Diuretic, laxative, tonic	Helps: ease wind and digestive problems, colic, constipation, bronchitis			

Because there are many aromatherapy essences, some of which are very expensive, we have selected a basic group that has a wide range of effects. As you become more familiar with the essences you can gradually add to your collection.

BASIC STROKES

In massage, the whole range of different strokes fall into four main groups: light gliding strokes; medium depth strokes; deep tissue, or friction strokes; and percussion. Once you have mastered these, you can begin to improvise and use them in a variety of different ways and combinations, developing your own personal style. Before using the massage strokes on a partner, practice them on your legs, so that you have some idea of how they feel and what their effects are. Make sure you are warm enough and sitting comfortably, and spend a few minutes centring yourself before you start (see p.19). Work very slowly at first and keep your awareness both in your hands and in the sensations you are receiving. Try to put your whole body behind your movements, not just your hands, and let them come from your *hara* and pelvis. See, also, if you can develop a rhythmical flow to the strokes as you practice. At a different time, try out the basic Shiatsu techniques (see p.27), which provide the essentials you need to learn before using Shiatsu as a healing tool.

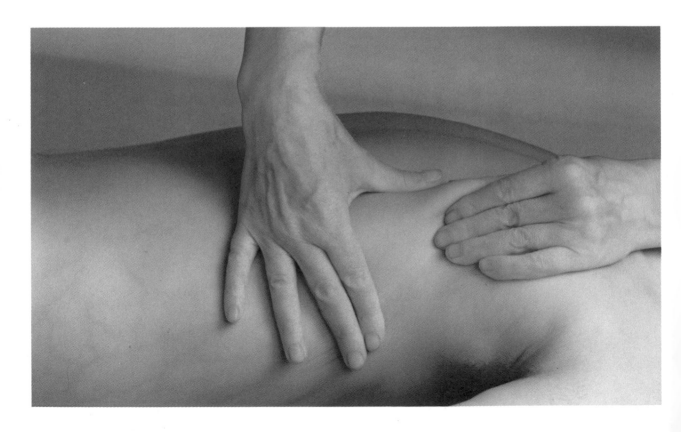

1 Long oiling strokes

Rest your oiled hands on the part of your partner's body you are about to work with. With your hands side by side and fingers together, glide smoothly away from yourself, reaching as far as you can go. Then divide your hands and draw back along the sides of the limb or torso, enfolding the area. Flow back to the original starting position and continue the cycle.

Gliding strokes

The long, light gliding and feathering strokes are used both at the beginning and at the end of a massage. With them you make the initial acquaintance with your partner's body. As you caringly spread the oil, you warm and energize an area of the body prior to working more deeply into it. The gliding strokes vary from light to firm, but should always be done slowly and with the whole of your hands flowing and moulding over the forms of the body. You can come back to these strokes at any time during a massage. The feathering is a long light trusting stroke that can connect a whole area – ideal for bidding farewell to a part of the body you have just worked with.

2 Circling

To spread oil more thoroughly or to stroke and soothe a wider area, make slow broad circles with your hands, using them simultaneously or alternately. Work slowly and rhythmically as you explore the terrain of your partner's body. Let the circles flow into each other in gentle spiralling movements.

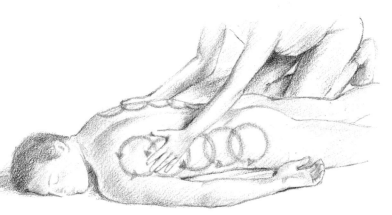

3 Feathering

Relax your hands and begin the lightest of brushing strokes with your fingertips, drawing your hands toward you, one after the other, with this stroke, which feels like feathers gently caressing the skin. Use it to connect a whole area as you prepare to take leave of it, or to change to a different stroke.

Medium depth strokes

These moderately deep strokes work more directly with the muscle masses. Sometimes circular, sometimes back and forth, they help to stimulate the circulation, which assists in clearing waste products more quickly from the muscles. They are also relaxing. Use a fairly bold and generous approach, allowing your body to rock gently behind the kneading, pulling or wringing. If you let the movements come from your pelvis rather than shoulders and arms it will be less tiring for you and more effective for your partner.

I Kneading

Use the whole of your hand to grasp and lift a bunch of flesh or muscle in a circular squeezing motion. Work your hands alternately with a rocking rhythmical movement, very much like kneading dough. Your hands can maintain a constant contact with the skin while doing this stroke.

2 Pulling

With one hand over the far side of the torso or of a limb, as shown right, slowly pull upward, lifting the muscle firmly as your hand follows the curve of the part and gently breaks contact. Before the contact is broken, start pulling a little further on with your other hand. Let your hands pull in a flowing movement, overlapping as they travel along.

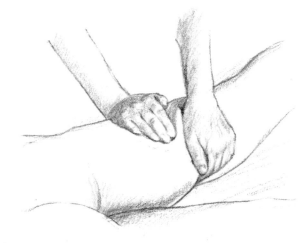

3 Wringing

Kneeling beside your partner, with your hands cupped over a limb, as shown left, slide the fingers of one hand right over to the far side, while the heel of your other hand comes down on the near side. Keeping your hands close together, repeat in the opposite direction. Continue in a steady back-and-forth movement, wringing either up or down the limb.

1 Thumb pressing

Place your thumbs on the soft tissue next to the bone at the edge of a joint. Keeping your arms straight, slowly lean forward from your hips so that your body weight builds up a gradual pressure on your thumbs. Hold, release, then move your thumbs a little and repeat. Continue to press all around the joint.

Deep tissue or friction strokes

The aim of these strokes is to penetrate into the deeper layers of muscles, into the connections of tendons and ligaments to bones and around joints. Thumbs and fingers are most commonly used for the friction strokes. Though appearing to circle or slide on the skin surface, they actually push in and direct pressure to the deeper levels below. The heel-of-the-hands stroke is a broader deep-tissue movement with quite a lot of power behind it. Go steadily and slowly, always staying very present. Never continue beyond the pain threshold.

2 Finger friction

With your fingers in the soft tissue between the bones of a joint, as shown right, apply fairly deep pressure to penetrate to the deeper structures within, and rotate your fingertips as you do so. Circling on the skin rather than sliding over it, try to focus your movement at a deeper level below the surface. Move all around the joint in this way.

3 Deep pressure with heel of hand

With the heels of your hands pressing into the flesh, as shown left, push slowly and firmly away from you, one hand behind the other. Create a deep rhythmical movement in which you alternately push away, lift off and come down again with the heel of one hand behind that of the hand in front.

Percussion strokes

This group of pounding or drumming strokes stimulates the skin and circulation and can relax tight muscles. But because of the vigorous and noisy nature of these movements they are often more appropriate if you want your massage to be stimulating rather than relaxing. You will need to experiment and decide this for yourself. Before beginning, shake your hands up and down for a few moments to relax your wrists. The blows themselves are light and bouncy – as if you are striking a rubber ball. Don't use percussion strokes on the spine or any other protruding bony area.

I Hacking

With the first three fingers of each hand together and your little ones slightly apart to act as shock absorbers, start a rapid up-and-down movement, keeping your wrists relaxed. Practice in the air, then let your hands come down in a series of light quick blows, travelling up and down along muscled areas.

2 Cupping

With your fingers fairly straight, cup your hands, as shown below, closing the sides with your thumbs, and begin to do the same brisk and rhythmically alternating sequence of strokes described in Step I. The position of the hand creates a slight vacuum with each blow, which results in a rather loud clapping noise on the skin.

3 Plucking

Gently pluck small portions of flesh between thumbs and fingers, as shown above, lifting and letting them slip from between your fingers in quick succession.

1 Shiatsu "Dragon's mouth" technique
Extend your thumbs and forefingers to stretch the connecting skin. Holding this shape place both hands over one of your partner's arms or legs, and apply pressure down through this part of your hands, keeping your arms straight and fingers and shoulders relaxed. You can also use this technique on the back of the neck (see Step 3, p.48).

2 Shiatsu palm and heel-of-hand pressure
Rest the palms of your hands on your partner's body, as shown below, and apply pressure as in Step 1. Lean into your hands to increase the pressure. For more precision of pressure, focus your body weight through the heels of your hands, while still keeping the rest of your hands in soft contact with your partner's body.

Basic techniques: Shiatsu

The application of pressure and stretching backed up by support forms the basis for most of the techniques used in Shiatsu. You create variety by using different parts of your body. We show three commonly used methods. Keep your shoulders relaxed, and your knees apart for stability. Focus on using your body weight in a controlled yet relaxed way, letting movements come from your hara. You should apply pressure as you both exhale. Keep both hands in contact with your partner – if one hand is active, let the other, the "mother hand", rest on the body. For clarity we have shown the receiver naked, but Shiatsu is normally done clothed.

3 Shiatsu thumb pressure
Place the pads of your thumbs on your partner's body, as shown above, your fingers spread and resting there lightly to balance you and to reassure your partner. Slowly lean your body weight over your thumbs to increase the pressure. Keep your arms straight, but not rigid. Build up pressure gradually, hold then release.

COMMON AILMENTS

This section consists of a series of strokes and techniques that can help bring comfort and healing to a variety of common ailments. Most of the techniques shown are massage strokes, but where we feel that they are especially effective,we have also included some Shiatsu techniques. The body chart on pages 30 and 31 will help you to locate specific problems and lead you to the respective treatment, where you can try the strokes suggested. It is a good idea to start by practicing the whole body massage (see pp.32-43) as this will familiarize you with the basic strokes and accustom you to using your own body correctly.

When working on the floor and moving around your partner stay aware of your own posture and be careful not to jolt him or her. Be sure to work in positions that are comfortable to you, as any discomfort in your own body will be transmitted to your partner. It may be worth investing in a table (see p.18), as this makes it easier to move freely around your partner.

Always begin by centring and then making a gentle contact with your partner's body (see pp.19-20), before starting to work slowly and sensitively with the strokes. Pleasure is conducive to healing, and a caring touch gives both encouragement and reassurance.

When you move on to strokes and techniques for ailments in specific parts of the body you should always begin with the basic oiling stroke for that part of the body, unless you are doing Shiatsu or clothed massage, when of course you won't be using oil. In Shiatsu you can begin by briefly making contact to allow the body to open to your touch before beginning the technique.

A certain degree of pain can feel welcome during a massage, especially when treating stiff or tense muscles. But you should always let pain be a guideline and never exceed your partner's pain threshold. Encourage your partner to tell you what feels particularly helpful and to let you know immediately if anything you do feels too tender. If any aches and pains are severe or persist in spite of the massage, encourage your partner to consult a doctor. This book is not intended to help you to diagnose ailments or offer instant "cures". You should only treat ailments that are not serious or those that have already been professionally diagnosed, and before beginning any of the following treatments you should read the advice on pages 90 to 93, on arthritis, sprains, strains and times when you should not massage. If you can bear these simple points in mind, caring touch can provide many physical and psychological benefits and help to mobilize your partner's own healing energies toward a quicker recovery.

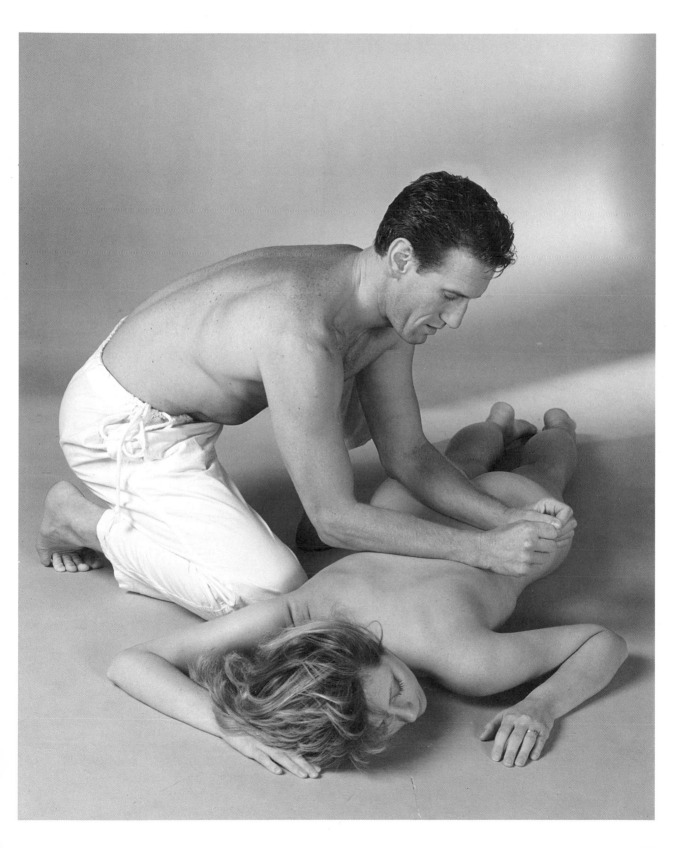

Where does it hurt?

To make it easier for you to find the relevant strokes and techniques, ailments are grouped under the part of the body chiefly affected. The parts of the body run in a sequence starting at the head and working down the body to the legs and feet.

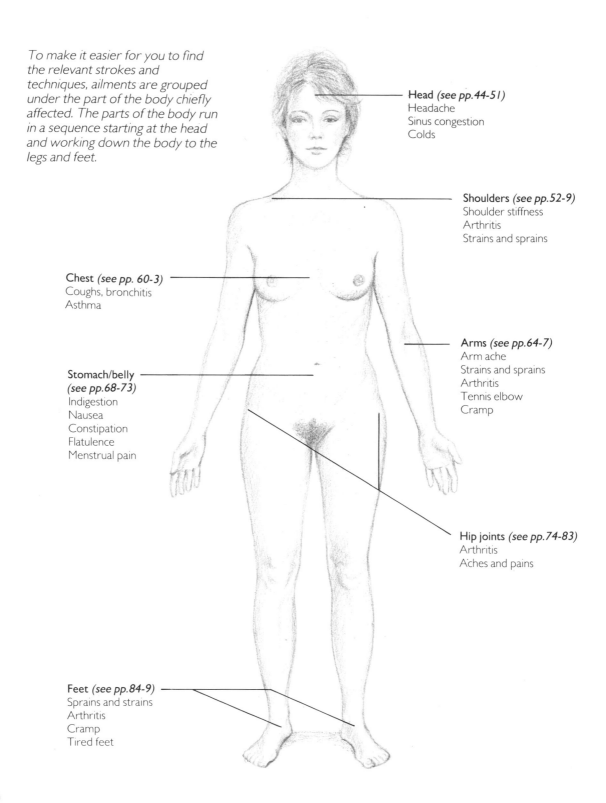

Head *(see pp.44-51)*
Headache
Sinus congestion
Colds

Shoulders *(see pp.52-9)*
Shoulder stiffness
Arthritis
Strains and sprains

Chest *(see pp. 60-3)*
Coughs, bronchitis
Asthma

Arms *(see pp.64-7)*
Arm ache
Strains and sprains
Arthritis
Tennis elbow
Cramp

Stomach/belly
(see pp.68-73)
Indigestion
Nausea
Constipation
Flatulence
Menstrual pain

Hip joints *(see pp.74-83)*
Arthritis
Aches and pains

Feet *(see pp.84-9)*
Sprains and strains
Arthritis
Cramp
Tired feet

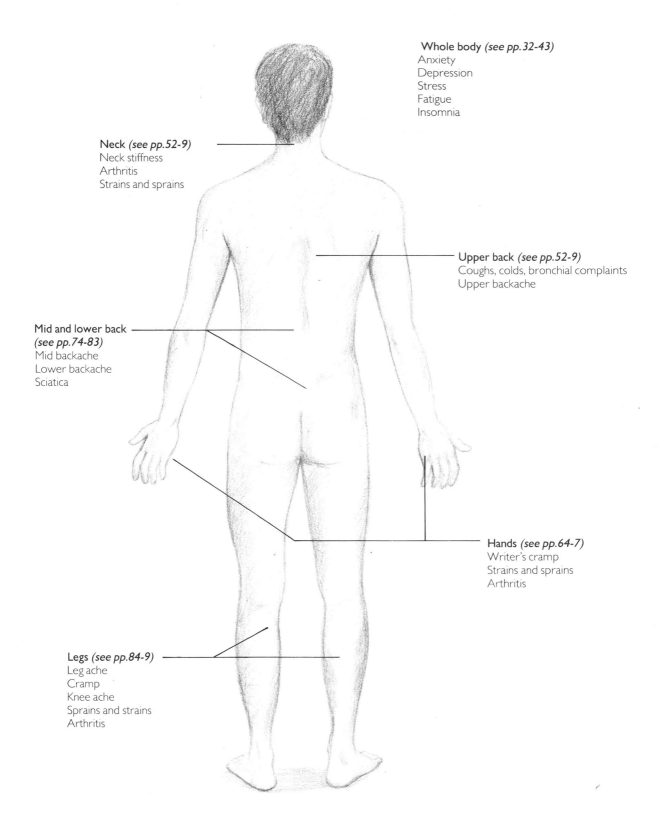

Whole body *(see pp. 32-43)*
Anxiety
Depression
Stress
Fatigue
Insomnia

Neck *(see pp. 52-9)*
Neck stiffness
Arthritis
Strains and sprains

Upper back *(see pp. 52-9)*
Coughs, colds, bronchial complaints
Upper backache

Mid and lower back
(see pp. 74-83)
Mid backache
Lower backache
Sciatica

Hands *(see pp. 64-7)*
Writer's cramp
Strains and sprains
Arthritis

Legs *(see pp. 84-9)*
Leg ache
Cramp
Knee ache
Sprains and strains
Arthritis

WHOLE BODY

A whole body massage can be a wonderfully nourishing and relaxing experience, good for body and soul. The overall benefits of massage, such as improved circulation, soothed nerves and relaxed muscles, and the general sense of well-being that results, make it a great way to maintain good health. Massaging the entire body also enhances body awareness, giving us a more complete body image and making us feel more whole. When we do succumb to the stresses and strains of life, then often a massage can help to restore the harmony that we have lost. The following sequence, which should take about one hour, takes you step by step through the whole body. It is just one possible way of doing a massage. As you become more familiar with the strokes and with giving massage you will develop your own sequences and discover many other techniques. Stay aware with your hands, and use them to "listen" to your partner's body. See if you can put your whole body behind your movements, and let them come from your *hara* (see p.19) and pelvis. Try, also, to regard the massage as a kind of dance or a piece of music. As you go, flow from one part of the body to another and develop your own natural rhythm.

Insomnia, fatigue, anxiety and depression

Mental and physical over-activity can lead to any or all of these complaints. They are our body's "warning signals". A caring massage, combined with essential oils, can supply the relaxing space that is needed. For insomnia you can use camomile essence (see p.21), for fatigue use bergamot, and for anxiety and mild depression use lavender. Before starting the massage, read the section on contraindications (see p.93).

Caution: *If you have deep depression or anxiety you should consult your doctor.*

1 Spreading oil on back

With your partner lying on her front, kneel at her head, oil your hands and let them rest on the centre of her upper back. Glide down alongside her spine with your fingers together and hands relaxed. Go forward from your hips, not just your shoulders. At the end of your reach divide your hands and glide back up her sides. Repeat several times.

2 Sliding up curve of shoulder

Choose the shoulder opposite to the way in which your partner is facing, as shown right, and glide one hand slowly across her upper back, then along the curve of shoulder and neck up to the base of her skull and off at the hairline. Let your other hand follow behind, alternating your hands in a continual rhythmic movement.

3 Working shoulder in strips

Place your thumbs on the side of your partner's neck, your fingers resting on her back, as shown left. Now glide your thumbs along the shoulder, in the channel between bone and muscle, and out toward the shoulder joint. Repeat, but each time work a little higher, covering the shoulder top in strips. Help your partner to turn her head and repeat from Step 2 on the other side.

4 Oiling buttocks
Sit at one of your partner's sides facing up toward her head. Oil your hands and let them come to rest on the sacrum (base of spine). Now glide up the centre of the lower back and circle your hands out and down to the sides of the body, draw back across the hips and circle around the buttocks and back to the sacrum. Repeat this stroke several times.

5 Circling lower back
Still facing up toward your partner's head, begin to make counter-clockwise circles with your right hand around the lower back while your left hand makes clockwise circles. Allow both to overlap. Apply more pressure as you pull in toward the centre of her back and down toward the buttocks. Let your hands move slowly.

6 Kneading buttocks and sides
Turn to face across your partner's side and reach over to the opposite buttock. With both hands, begin to knead the muscles with firm generous squeezing and lifting strokes. Continue kneading right up the side of the body to the shoulder and back down again. Repeat on the other side.

7 Oiling backs of legs
Sit or kneel at one of your partner's feet and rest your oiled hands at the back of her ankle and lower calf. Then gliding slowly up the leg to the top of her thigh, divide your hands, one branching out around the hip joint and the other down the inside of the thigh. Avoid going too close to the genitals. Then, with both hands enfolding her leg, draw right down to the foot, across the sole and off at the toes. Repeat.
Caution: Avoid using any of the leg strokes on varicose veins (see p.93).

8 "Draining" back of leg
With both hands cupped, start an alternating stroke that pushes slowly up the back of the whole leg from ankle to thigh. Keep all your fingers in contact with the sides of the leg, and let your hands glide upward in a series of rhythmical strokes. Check with your partner for pressure and make sure you "drain" both back and sides of the thigh thoroughly.

9 Wringing down back of leg
Move around to kneel beside your partner's thigh and rest both your hands at the top of the thigh. Then wring your hands slowly and firmly back and forth in opposite directions (see p.24), stretching the tissue in between them. Let each of your hands simultaneously touch the work surface on either side of the leg before wringing across again. Move down the leg to the ankle.

10 Lifting lower leg

Sit or kneel facing sideways on to your partner's leg and, with one hand just above the back of her knee, lift the lower leg with the other hand to a vertical position.

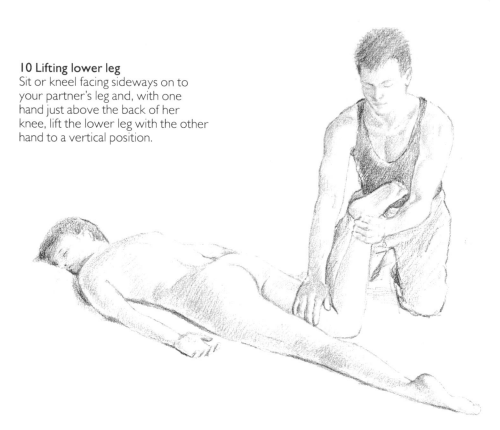

11 Loosening ankle joint

Using both your fingers and thumbs, start to work with slow sensitive strokes on either side of the ankle, as shown below, pushing into the soft tissue between the bones with small stroking and circling movements. Stay focused, and travel right around the joint in this way.

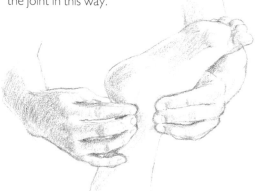

12 Thumbing sole

Clasp both hands around the foot, as shown above, and let your thumbs rest on the sole. Using your thumbs, push and slowly circle all the way along the sole from the heel to the toes, exploring every hill and hollow as you go. Repeat from Step 7 on the other leg.

13 Neck and shoulder cycle

Ask your partner to turn over, and kneel at her head. Turn her head to rest on one of your cupped hands, her cheek upward and her chin toward her collar bone. Let your free hand rest on the upper chest, fingers toward the centre, heel of the hand facing out toward the shoulder. Draw slowly out toward the shoulder joint and curve your hand around it . . .

. . . then, with a firm slow pressure push in with the flats of your fingers along the curve of shoulder and neck, as shown left, drawing your hand slowly right up the back of the neck to the base of her skull. Let your fingers slide along the rim of bone until only the tips are in contact . . .

. . . then rotate your hand so that your fingers point down toward the centre of your partner's chest again, and slide your whole hand down, as shown right, into the "V" shape made where the collar bone joins the long neck muscle, and then on to the chest. Avoid the throat. Then repeat the whole cycle several times. Turn your partner's head and work the sequence on the other side.

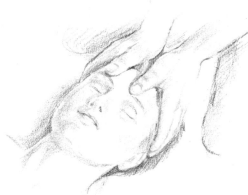

14 Stroking forehead

Sit at your partner's head and rest your thumbs on the centre of her forehead. Now with your hands supporting the sides of the head, slowly draw your thumbs away from the centre, as shown left, to the hairline, and off. Repeat this stroke several times.

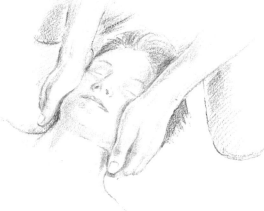

15 Massaging cheeks

With the heels of both your hands resting on the cheeks close to and on either side of the nose, and your fingers pointing down toward the ears, slide your hands slowly out across the sides of the face until you reach the ears, as shown right.

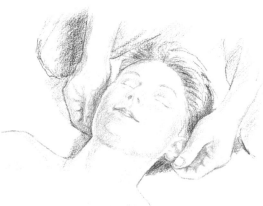

16 Stretching and squeezing ears

Now gently grasp the ears between fingers and thumbs and stretch them slightly outward and downward. Then spend some time squeezing and massaging the ears, exploring all the little crannies and crevices, as shown left.

17 Clearing along jaw bone

Gently squeeze the tip of the chin with your thumbs and fingers and then slowly draw them out along the jaw bone in a long firm stroke, tracing the whole length of the rim of the bone to the ears, as shown right.

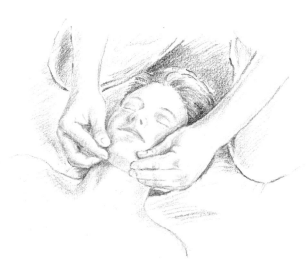

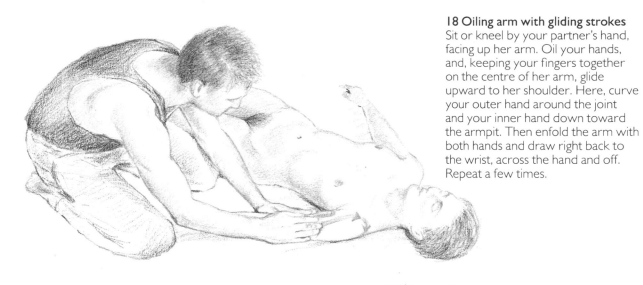

18 Oiling arm with gliding strokes

Sit or kneel by your partner's hand, facing up her arm. Oil your hands, and, keeping your fingers together on the centre of her arm, glide upward to her shoulder. Here, curve your outer hand around the joint and your inner hand down toward the armpit. Then enfold the arm with both hands and draw right back to the wrist, across the hand and off. Repeat a few times.

19 "Draining" arm

With her palm facing upward, hold one of your partner's wrists, and with your free hand begin to squeeze her arm between your thumb and fingers all the way along from the wrist as far as you can reach. Break contact at the top and start at the wrist again. Try to cover a different strip each time.

20 Spreading thumbs down arm

Clasp your partner's upper arm with both hands, your thumbs together in the centre. Squeezing with your whole hand, draw your thumbs outward to spread the flesh. Now slide a little way down and bring your thumbs together again to squeeze out once more. Continue like this all the way down the arm to the wrist.

21 Thumbing on palm
With your partner's palm facing upward, lift her hand and work on it with your thumbs, making slow circles and squeezing and pressing into the whole of the palm area.

22 Spreading palms and fingers
Interlock your fingers between your partner's, as shown left, then gently open out the hand, spreading and stretching both the palm and fingers. Ask your partner to let you know when the stretch feels enough.

23 Stretching fingers
Hold your partner's hand palm downward in one hand, as shown right. Now take hold of one of her fingers at the point where it joins on to her hand and, squeezing the sides firmly, slide slowly down the finger, stretching it as you go. Let the pressure ease off as you reach the tip and slide off. Repeat on each finger and also the thumb. Repeat from Step 18 on the other side.

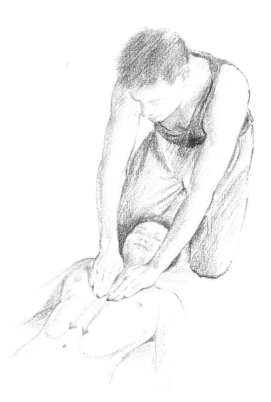

24 Oiling torso with gliding strokes
Sit or kneel at your partner's head and let your oiled hands float gently down to rest on her upper chest. With your hands together glide slowly down the centre of the body, divide your hands, then glide back up the sides and back to where you started. Repeat. (When working on the front of the torso, work around the breasts, not directly on them.)

25 Pulling up side of ribs
Start with one hand on the base of one side of your partner's ribcage. Glide up the side of the ribs, and on up the front of the chest. Let both your hands follow each other in this flowing stroke, each time starting higher up. Finally, pull up the side of the torso beneath the breast to the armpit. Repeat on the other side.

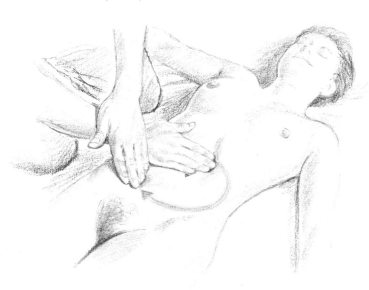

26 Circling around belly
Moving to your partner's side, let both hands come to rest very gently on the abdomen and pause there for a moment or two. Then, using both your hands, start to make slow, broad circling movements in a clockwise direction. One of your hands remains constantly on the body while the other gently breaks contact once in each cycle.

27 Oiling legs with gliding strokes

Kneel at your partner's feet and place your oiled hands on the front of her leg at the ankle. With your fingers together in the centre, glide up the leg to the top of the thigh and divide your hands outward, letting one go around the hip joint and the other curve down the inside of the thigh. Then enfold her leg and draw right down to the foot and off at the toes. Repeat.

28 "Draining" leg

With your fingers and thumbs curved over the leg in a "V" shape, push upward with alternating strokes, pressing the muscles on either side of the shin bone, around the knee joint, and along the sides and front of the thigh right to the top of the leg.

29 Enfolding foot

Place one of your hands on your partner's sole and the other on the top of her foot. Now slide your hands in a warm enfolding stroke slowly along top and bottom until your fingertips slide off the tips of her toes. Repeat a few times and then move to the other leg and repeat the whole sequence from Step 27.

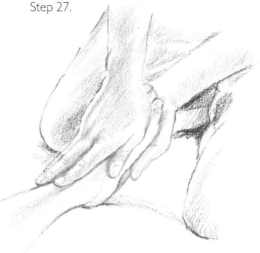

Connecting

At the end of a massage it always feels good to the receiver to have some long flowing strokes that link together all the parts of the body and give a sense of wholeness. Keep your touch light, but don't skip little bits as this will detract from the sense of completeness. Also, make sure that you travel to the very ends of the extremities of your partner's body. Another way of connecting is to link up any two parts of the body your hands feel drawn to. Finally, slowly break contact, gently cover your partner with a large warm towel, and leave her to rest and enjoy the feeling of relaxation for a while.

1 Connecting two parts
Sitting or kneeling at your partner's side, let one of your hands come to rest lightly on the belly and the other on the forehead. With your eyes closed just stay quietly in contact as you link body and head. Focus on your hands and the rhythm of your partner's breath. After a time, very slowly take your hands away.

2 Connecting strokes
Using middle and ring fingers of each hand, rest them on your partner's forehead. Then glide over the top of her head, down the back of her neck, along the shoulders, down the arms to the fingertips and off. Return to the forehead and repeat, but from the back of her neck come around to the front of the upper chest and then glide down, dividing at the belly and travelling down the legs to the tips of the toes and off.

HEAD

The head is the main control centre of the body, and in the protective cave of the skull lies the amazing brain – a vastly complex and mysterious organ. The head is also the seat of two of the *chakras*, or energy centres (see p.12), found along the centre line of the body. The Crown *chakra*, at the top of the head, is related to our essence and spirituality, and the Pineal or Brow *chakra*, at the centre of the forehead, is related to clear seeing, intuition and intellect. In a head-oriented culture, we sometimes find our mind racing and overloaded. Instead of clarity of thought we experience confusion and weariness. The result of this is often a headache. There are a variety of other causes for headaches – one of the commonest is stress, which can create tension in the muscles of the neck, shoulders and scalp. Other types of headache include those resulting from sinus congestion, colds or flu; menstrual-related headaches; headaches following whiplash or neck injury; and migraines – recurring, throbbing headaches, which may be accompanied by nausea or vomiting. Both massage and Shiatsu have effective treatments for headaches and head congestion, so in the following pages we have included helpful sequences from both.

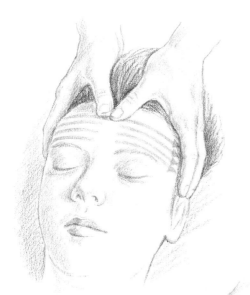

Headaches: massage

Since it is hard to distinguish between the different types of headaches, several massage sequences are given in the following pages and it is a good idea to try all the different strokes, focusing on those that seem to give your partner most comfort. On this page the receiver is lying down, and on pages 46 and 47 sitting up. The series of strokes on page 47 is a soothing and relaxing sequence taken from an ancient Indian healing massage. Camomile and lavender essences are both helpful for headaches (see p.21). Melissa is good for migraines and

Continued overleaf

1 Working forehead in strips

Kneel at your partner's head and rest your thumbs in the centre of her forehead just above her eyebrows, with your fingers around the sides of her head. Slowly and firmly draw your thumbs away from the centre, out toward the temples, the hairline and off. Work like this in strips right up the forehead until you cover the whole area.

2 Pressing and circling temples

Begin by pressing on your partner's temples, for ten seconds or so, with the flats of your fingers. Then slowly release the pressure and make slow circles over both the temples. Check with your partner whether she'd like a deeper or lighter touch.

3 Base of skull pressure

Turn your partner's head to rest comfortably on one hand, with her cheek facing upward. Using the fingertips of your free hand, push up and under the bone of the skull base. Hold, letting the pressure build up, then slowly release. Work right along the rim, searching out tense spots, then turn the head to the other side and repeat.

Continued from p.45

the stroke in Step 2 which circles the temples, may be particularly beneficial. It is also helpful to lie in a darkened room and apply a cold compress (see p.91) to the forehead. Many headaches will also respond well to the sequence given in Shoulders, Neck and Upper back (see pp.54-9). If you have had a whiplash injury and keep getting headaches, or if you have pain in your arm, it would be wise to see an osteopath or doctor to check for joint damage.

Caution*: If a headache comes on suddenly, is severe, and is accompanied by a very stiff neck or back, a fever, weakness in a limb, drowsiness or confusion, loss of vision and/or epileptic fits, seek medical help and advice at once.*

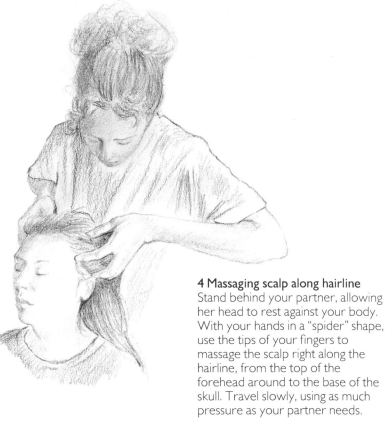

4 Massaging scalp along hairline

Stand behind your partner, allowing her head to rest against your body. With your hands in a "spider" shape, use the tips of your fingers to massage the scalp right along the hairline, from the top of the forehead around to the base of the skull. Travel slowly, using as much pressure as your partner needs.

5 Pressing and circling jaw muscles

Rest the pads of your fingers on the jaw muscles. If you have difficulty finding them, rest your fingers on the cheeks and ask your partner to clench and unclench her teeth, which causes these muscles to rise and fall. Now begin to press and circle your fingers over the whole area of the jaw muscles. Work slowly and thoroughly to release tension.

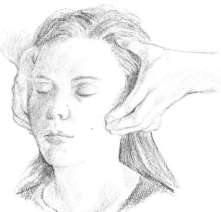

6 Fingertip healing

Ask your partner to focus on her breath and let your fingertips come to rest very lightly in two vertical lines on either side of her forehead, above the middle of her eyebrows. Keep your shoulders relaxed, focus on your *hara* and maintain a light steady contact for a few minutes.

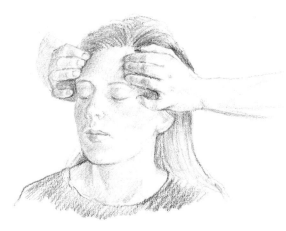

7 Stroking over top of head
Rest the middle and ring fingers of one hand on the middle of the forehead and those of the other in the hollow at the centre base of the skull. Now lightly stroke your fingers from the forehead up and across the centre line of the skull and down to meet the fingers at the base. Then pull both hands out and away from the body as if draining tension away from the back of the head. Repeat.

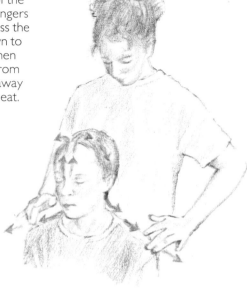

9 Stroking around hairline
Begin as before, your fingers touching at the centre of your partner's forehead. Then stroke gently straight up to her hairline. Divide your hands and draw your fingers right along the hairline, curve above the ears and around the rim of the skull to the centre base. When your fingers meet at the centre, pull them back away from the head as before. Repeat several times.

8 Stroking head to shoulders
Stand behind your partner and gently rest the same fingers of each hand on the centre of her forehead. Draw your fingers lightly up to the top of the head then divide your hands, coming down the sides of the head behind the ears, down the sides of the neck, along the tops of the shoulders, and off. Repeat the movement several times.

10 Face massage sequence
Starting at the centre of the forehead, and using the same fingers of each hand, stroke down and then out and right around each eye, down alongside the nose, then around the mouth, letting your fingers meet under the lower lip. Continue down to the chin tip then along the jaw bone, up and over the ears, along the rim of the skull to the centre base and off. Repeat a few times.

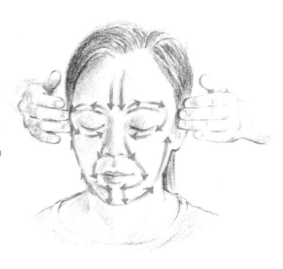

Headaches: Shiatsu

*Headaches are frequently caused
by poor digestion and inadequate
elimination of toxins. Most of the
meridians concerned with these
functions run through the neck,
shoulders, and upper back and any
imbalances can affect different
parts of the head. Working around
the upper back, shoulders and
neck, as shown here, will release
stagnant energy in the appropriate
meridians and help relieve
headaches. Pressing* tsubos *on the
meridian lines in other parts of the
body, such as feet, legs, hands,
arms and shoulders, can also help
to relieve pain in the head, as in
Step 6. If the* tsubos *are painful,
hold them with light pressure, and
agitate the point slightly in a
comfortable way.*

1 Shiatsu scalp massage
Bring your partner's head forward
and support her forehead in your
cupped palm. With your free hand
begin to massage the whole of the
scalp, using your thumbs and fingers
in a slow shampooing motion that
travels over the whole area. Focus
your attention on the parts of the
scalp that feel most tender to her.

2 Shiatsu neck stretch
Support your partner from behind,
with your elbows resting on the
front of her shoulders, ease them
slightly back. Place your hands on the
back of her head while her head
sinks forward to the point of
resistance. Hold for up to 30
seconds, while she breathes deeply.
Do not apply strong pressure.

3 Shiatsu neck side roll
With your partner's head still
forward, cup her forehead with one
hand and let the other support the
back of the neck between stretched
thumb and forefinger. Now slowly
tilt the head back to rest on the hand
supporting the neck and begin to roll
it gently in a semi-circle from side to
side. Finally return the head to an
upright position.

4 Shiatsu heel-of-hand massage
Stand beside your partner and place one of your hands on her upper chest. With the heel of your other hand, make firm circling and vibrating movements all over the area between the spine and the shoulder blade and up on to the muscles at the top of the shoulder. Reverse your position and repeat on the other side.

5 Shiatsu pressing top of shoulders
Stand behind your partner and place the balls of your thumbs on top of her shoulders, near to the neck, as shown below right. Use your body weight to apply pressure gradually, hold for a few seconds, then release slowly. Repeat the technique, moving outward along the shoulder, working the soft tissue between the bones.

6 Shiatsu connecting points
Kneel, with one knee up, beside your partner. With one hand on her shoulder, use your other thumb and forefinger to squeeze gently into the fleshy part between the bones of her thumb and her forefinger. Meanwhile, press into the small indentation on the outside of the shoulder bone with your thumb. Hold for up to 30 seconds. Continue, using your thumbs, with light pressure, to connect up any points that are tender, as indicated in the illustration left.

Sinus congestion

The sinuses are air spaces in the skull that connect with the cavity inside the nose, and when the mucous membranes of the nose are inflamed or congested, the tiny passageways into the sinuses become blocked. This can lead to discomfort and inflammation in the sinuses, and may cause aching in the face or a headache. The following sequence works around and across the bones where the sinuses are located and should be done slowly and sensitively, with your partner lying down. Check that the amount of pressure you are using feels right. Use either marjoram or lavender essence here (see p.21).

1 Pressing around eye socket

With your partner lying down, rest the tips of your forefingers under the rims of her upper eye sockets, by her nose. Now push up and under the bones, build up pressure, hold and release. Move a step outward and repeat. Circle both eye sockets, using your thumbs to press the lower sockets.

2 Clearing cheek bones

Begin with your thumbs on the cheek bones, just below the eyes and next to the nose. Slowly and firmly sweep out in a curving line that travels out to the hairline and away. Move down a little way and repeat the stroke. Work in this way in strips down the cheek bones from side of nose to hairline, until you reach the base of the cheek bones.

3 Pressing under cheek bones

Using the tips of the first two fingers of each hand, start close to the sides of the nose, and press up under the rim of each cheek bone. Gradually build pressure, hold, then release. Move a step outward on each side and repeat the pressure. Continue along the edge of the bone until you get to the ears.

Colds

The common cold is a virus infection, and the probability of catching colds rises when your natural resistance is lowered. All you can really do is let a cold run its course. A face and head massage can help to clear congestion; any of the sequences in this section on the head may be useful. The two Shiatsu techniques shown work on the tsubos, *which help to clear congestion and aid elimination of mucus, and the In-Do point on the forehead, which relieves heaviness in the head caused both by colds and sinus problems. Rosemary or eucalyptus essences may be helpful (see p.21).*

I Self-help oil rub

Use eucalyptus or rosemary essence (see p.21). Gently massage the oil into the whole area around your nose and sinuses. If you have a chesty cold, apply it to your upper chest as well. Use small, deep circling movements to rub the oil quite thoroughly into the skin.

3 Shiatsu In-Do point

Kneel and ask your partner to lie down, supporting her head on your knees. Place your middle fingertips, one resting on the other, between and very slightly higher than the eyebrows. With light pressure, move the skin sensitively in tiny circles over this *tsubo.* Use your lower fingertip to "sense" while the upper one subtly creates the movement.

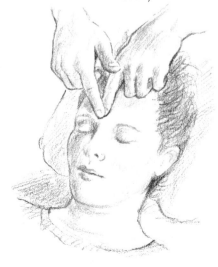

2 Shiatsu lung *tsubos*

Stand behind your partner, and let her lean against you. Curve both your hands over her shoulder joints so that your fingertips rest in the valleys between her shoulders and chest. Now move your fingers slightly forward on to the muscles and massage in small circles, applying pressure with your fingertips.

51

NECK, SHOULDERS AND UPPER BACK

Bridging the head and the shoulders, the neck is a busy junction where a huge amount of activity takes place. Major blood vessels in the neck link the body to the head. The spinal nerves travel through the vertebrae of the neck and on down the spine, carrying messages between the brain and all other parts of the body. And the throat houses the voice-box, as well as the passages for food and air. The shoulder joints have the widest range of movement in the body, and the whole shoulder and neck area can be easily strained by overuse, unwise lifting or sudden jarring movements. When we are under stress, it is the shoulder and neck muscles that tend to hold tension the most. This area also links with the Throat *chakra* (see p.12), which relates to the expression of feelings via arm or body movements, or through the voice. "Heart" feelings (see Heart *chakra* p.12) are also expressed through the arms. When we bottle up our feelings we actually tighten muscles in the throat, shoulder and chest area to hold them in. Tense raised shoulders can reflect fear, being the posture of the "startle reflex" when we galvanize ourselves to meet some real or imagined threat. For all these reasons this area often causes us discomfort.

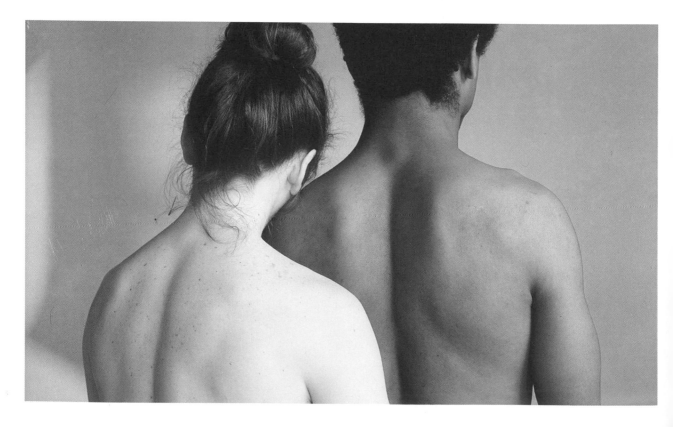

Neck stiffness, arthritis and strain

Stiffness in the neck may be caused by sleeping in an awkward position, or from getting very cold, from straining muscles or ligaments, by sudden jarring movements, or simply from being anxious. When applying the following massage strokes, keep your touch gentle but firm, always remain within the threshold of pain, and go slowly. If your partner has arthritis of the neck (see p.92) omit Steps 4 and 8, p.54-5. Try rosemary essence (see p.21). Compresses (see p.91) can also be helpful for neckache.

I Stroking and stretching back of neck

With your partner lying on her back use both hands alternately to stroke up the back of the neck from base to skull. Then cup your hands under the back of the head and pull toward you, stretching the neck. Make sure your thumbs don't drag on the ears. Now glide your hands along the back of the head and slide off at the top.

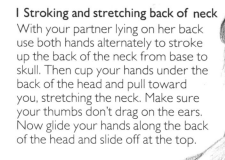

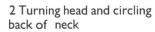

2 Turning head and circling back of neck

First cup both your hands around and under your partner's skull, with your thumbs resting in front of the ears. Then slightly lift and gently turn the head to rest on one of your cupped hands. Check that the position feels comfortable. Now use your free hand to massage the back of the neck in slow firm circles, moving right up to the skull base.

3 Kneading muscle at base of neck

Slide your hand down one side of the neck and grasp the muscle at the top of the shoulder between your fingers and thumb. Slowly squeeze and knead the muscle, pushing your fingers underneath it with circling movements to reach different parts. Ask your partner to say what feels particularly good. Repeat from Step 2 on the other side.

4 Stretching side of neck
Cup one of your hands under your partner's skull and draw her head sideways toward her shoulder. Now use your free hand, fingers pointing toward the floor, to glide down the side of the neck and along the shoulder to the top of the shoulder joint, as shown. Press firmly down toward her hand, stretching the side of the neck between your two hands. Then glide back up the shoulder and neck and repeat the stretch twice more. Now reverse your hands and stretch the other side of the neck.

5 Stretching neck forward and backward
Cup both your hands under your partner's skull and slowly lift her head forward, chin toward chest, to the point of resistance, as shown left. Bring her head down again and repeat. Now cup one hand under the skull, the other on top of her head, fingers pointing toward the floor, as shown below. Tilt the head right back so the chin comes up as high as possible. Release and stretch again. Then bring her head gently back to rest.

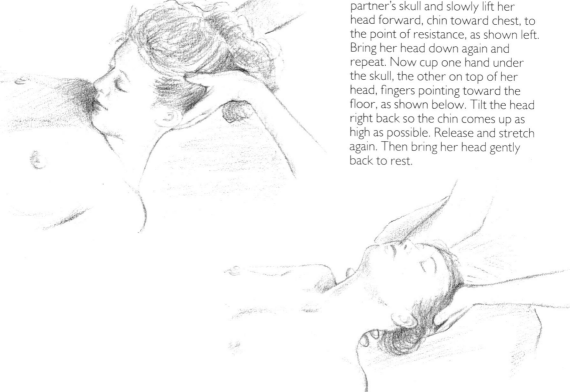

6 Self-help for arthritis and aching neck
Put two tennis balls into a sock and knot the end. Lie down with the balls at the top of your neck, just below the rim of your skull, one on each side. Do this for about five minutes a day. It can be very soothing for aching necks or osteoarthritis.

Caution: If you feel dizzy or experience pain, stop at once.

7 Neck massage with partner sitting
Let your partner sit at a table, supporting her head with her hands. Gently squeeze and stroke the back and sides of her neck with rhythmical movements. Move slowly, letting your partner be your guide for the amount of pressure needed. Try also massaging the upper shoulders and base of the neck with slow, firm kneading strokes, as this is a continuation of the neck muscle.

8 Rotating the neck
Stand behind your seated partner and put your wrist under her chin, your hand cradling her cheek. Cup the opposite side of her head with your other hand. Now slowly turn the head by simultaneously pulling the cheek and pushing against the side of the head until you reach the point of resistance. Release the head a little, and then take it back to the resistance point two more times. Then reverse the positions of your two hands and repeat the stroke on the other side.

1 Circling shoulder blade

Kneel at your partner's side, facing her head. Lift her hand on to her lower back and cup your outermost hand under her shoulder. Now cup your free hand over the top of the shoulder, close to the neck, and firmly lift the muscle. Then continue down along the edge of the shoulder blade, pushing in under the rim. Circle around the blade and back to the top of the shoulder. Repeat several times.

Upper back and shoulder stiffness or pain

Stiffness in the upper back can be caused by muscle strain or arthritis. Emotional stress can also cause tightness in the muscles, as can spending long hours sitting at a desk or making repetitive arm movements. In Shiatsu, the upper back relates to the lungs and heart, so by working here you can influence these organs and help treat such ailments as asthma or bronchial complaints. Try bergamot or rosemary essence here (see p.21). Muscular pain in this area can also be eased using compresses (see p.91).

Caution: *Before treating arthritic or injured joints see pp:90-3.*

2 Pressing flat of blade and squeezing along ridge

With the heel of your free hand, push slowly and firmly up the flat of the blade from base to top until your hand meets the ridge of bone running along the top of the blade. Clasp your fingers around the top of the ridge and squeeze your hand out toward the shoulder joint. Repeat the whole movement several times.

3 Rotating shoulder joint

Cup your outermost hand under your partner's shoulder joint, while your other hand holds her upper arm just above the elbow. Now start to lift and rotate the shoulder joint in a large slow circle, going to the point of resistance all the way around. After several circulations change direction and rotate the shoulder the other way. Repeat on the other side from Step 1.

4 "Sandwiching" out to shoulder joint

With your partner lying on her back, sit at her side facing toward her shoulders. Place one hand under her upper back at the base of the neck and the other hand on the centre of her chest, just below the collar bone. Slowly and firmly draw your hands toward you, squeezing out toward the shoulder joint. Repeat the stroke several times.

5 Kneading top of shoulder and joint

Begin to do some broad strokes from the neck along the top of the shoulder toward the joint. Use both hands alternately to squeeze and stroke along the muscle, and then spend some time working slowly around the joint, pressing into the soft tissue between the bones with your thumbs and fingers.

6 Stretching shoulder joint

Kneel by your partner's side, facing toward her head. Take hold of her wrist and hand between both of yours, with your thumbs in her palm. Now lift her arm and stretch it away from you up and out above her head. Release the pressure and then stretch again two or three times. Let the arm down to rest by the side and then repeat the stroke on the other side from Step 4.

7 Pulling up along spinal muscles

Sit at your partner's head and push both hands about a hand's length under the back on either side of the spine. Press up with the pads of your fingers into the muscles close to each side of the spine, then slowly draw your hands up along these muscles to the base of the neck, ironing out knots of tension. (See vertical arrows below.) Repeat several times.

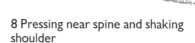

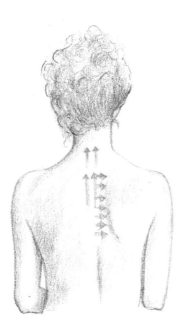

8 Pressing near spine and shaking shoulder

Sit facing your partner's side, at shoulder level. Push both hands under the shoulder blade until your fingertips reach the spine, as shown below left. With the pads of your fingers slowly press up into the muscles close to the spine. Press different areas alongside the upper spine. Now pull your hands toward you, to the rim of the shoulder blade (see horizontal arrows left) and lift and shake the whole shoulder quite vigorously, as shown below right. Repeat on the other side.

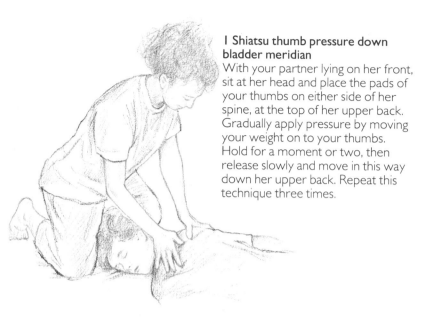

1 Shiatsu thumb pressure down bladder meridian

With your partner lying on her front, sit at her head and place the pads of your thumbs on either side of her spine, at the top of her upper back. Gradually apply pressure by moving your weight on to your thumbs. Hold for a moment or two, then release slowly and move in this way down her upper back. Repeat this technique three times.

Upper back stiffness and pain: Shiatsu

Deep pressure down the bladder meridians in the upper back will relax this whole area and will affect the functioning of the lungs and heart. Weakness in the front of the shoulders often causes tightness in the upper back meridians and muscles. These stretching techniques will open the upper chest and help relieve this stiffness. The back needs to be seen as a whole, however, since pain in the upper back can also be caused by lumbar problems. Whenever possible treat the mid and lower back areas too.

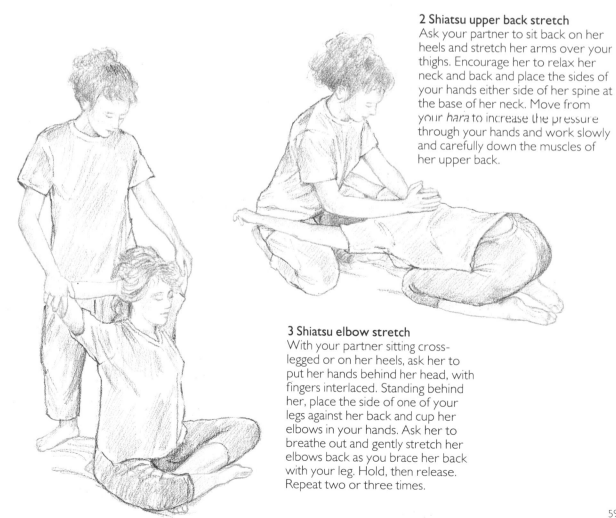

2 Shiatsu upper back stretch

Ask your partner to sit back on her heels and stretch her arms over your thighs. Encourage her to relax her neck and back and place the sides of your hands either side of her spine at the base of her neck. Move from your *hara* to increase the pressure through your hands and work slowly and carefully down the muscles of her upper back.

3 Shiatsu elbow stretch

With your partner sitting cross-legged or on her heels, ask her to put her hands behind her head, with fingers interlaced. Standing behind her, place the side of one of your legs against her back and cup her elbows in your hands. Ask her to breathe out and gently stretch her elbows back as you brace her back with your leg. Hold, then release. Repeat two or three times.

CHEST

The chest is the emotional centre of the body, housing our Heart *chakra* (see p.12), which relates to compassion, love and self-development. It is also the centre of breathing and if our chest is not constricted by tension, the ribcage expands and contracts freely as we inhale and exhale. Any tension in the chest area will restrict the breath and hence limit the amount of oxygen that we take in and use. Chest problems are often due to bottling up feelings – hence the expression "get it off your chest". Asthma attacks, though often an allergic reaction, may also be triggered by anxiety and upset. Those who suffer from chest problems can try cutting down dairy produce (thought to create mucus) and those who smoke should give it up. The following pages contain strokes that will help loosen mucus from the chest, and others that will aid and deepen the breathing. When massaging this area, bear in mind that the front of the body is more vulnerable and "open" than the back. Before beginning, rest both hands gently on your partner's chest and tune in to the breathing rhythm. If your partner is undressed, oil and soothe the chest first, using the strokes from the whole body massage (see p. 41).

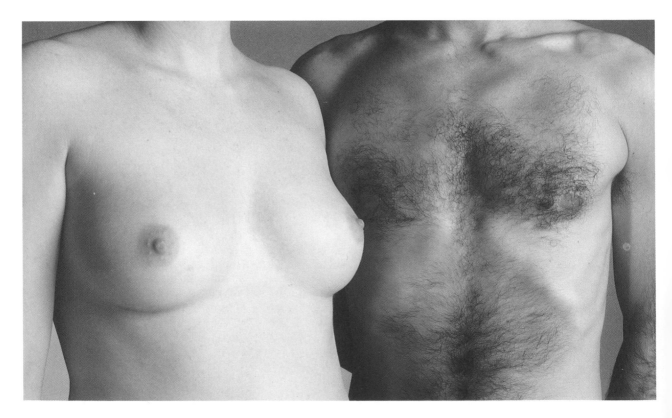

Chest congestion

These strokes will help to relieve any tension in the chest caused by bronchial infections and asthma. Easing the muscles alongside the spine will affect the nerves leading to all the organs of the chest. Try bergamot or eucalyptus essences here (see p.21). The percussion strokes create vibration in the chest cavity and lungs and can help to loosen mucus and phlegm from the bronchial tubes. For these (Steps 2 and 3) your partner needs a cushion under his belly so that his upper body is lower than his hips.

I Pushing muscles at side of spine

Kneel up, facing your partner's side. Leaning from your hips, place the heels of your hands just beyond the far edge of the spine at the top. Let your weight press down as you slide your hands outward across the ridge of muscle. Repeat this stroke, moving slowly down to the base of the ribs. Repeat on the other side.

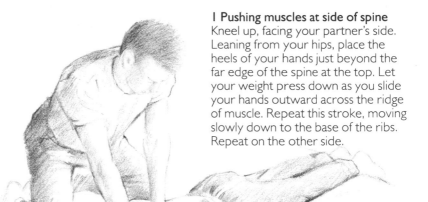

2 Cupping on ribs

Put your hands into a cupped position (see p.26). Then, with loose wrists, begin a rapid alternating clapping stroke over the whole far side of your partner's ribcage, from bottom to top and back again. Avoid working directly on the spine itself. Cupping on the upper back area affects the upper lobes of the lungs. Change sides and repeat on the other side of the chest.

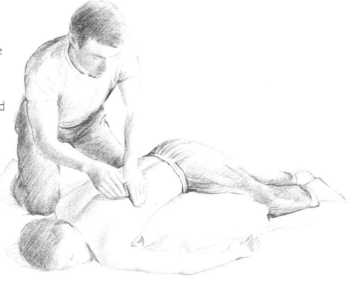

3 Thumping alongside spine

Place the flats of your fingers on the ridge of muscle nearest to you, at the side of the spine. Starting at the mid back, thump the back of your fingers quite rapidly, with your other hand in a loose fist, while sliding your fingers up alongside the spine (not directly on it), until you reach the base of the neck. Then thump down to the start again. Adapt your pressure to your partner's wishes. Repeat on the other side.

Breathing exercise for chest problems

This is a breathing exercise that derives from bioenergetics, and although it is accompanied here by a partner, it can be equally effective done by yourself. Rocking the pelvis as you breathe helps to exaggerate healthy respiratory movements. The movement also helps you to fill and empty the lungs fully. Here we give instructions separately for giver and receiver, but it is up to the giver to keep time with the receiver, and not the other way around.

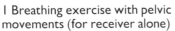

1 Breathing exercise with pelvic movements (for receiver alone)

Lie on your back, with your knees up and feet shoulder-width apart. Inhale, rocking your pelvis back so that your sacrum presses into the floor and your lower back hollows (see receiver in illustration above). Then exhale fully, letting your pelvis swing forward in the opposite direction, so that your tail bone lifts a little way off the floor (see receiver below). Repeat several times, then rest.

2 Co-ordinating stroke (for giver)

Sit at your partner's hips and watch his breathing pattern. Place your hands on his belly. As he inhales, glide up the centre of his body to the top of the chest and over the shoulders (see above), and as he exhales slide your hands down the sides of his chest, applying some pressure as air is expelled (see below). Repeat several times.

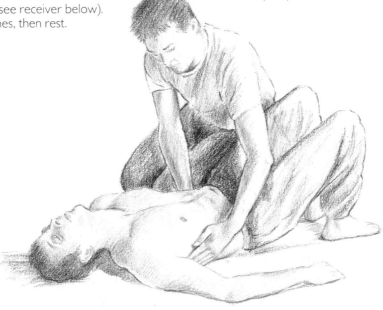

Coughs, bronchitis and asthma: Shiatsu

Circulatory and respiratory functions take place in the chest and Shiatsu will increase the energy to these two vital systems, encouraging the elimination of toxins and mucus. Rounded shoulders and a hunched back are indications that the person is protecting a weak chest. Work with care and respect as this area is the centre of emotions and can be vulnerable in many people. The technique shown in Step 2 should not be used on asthma sufferers.

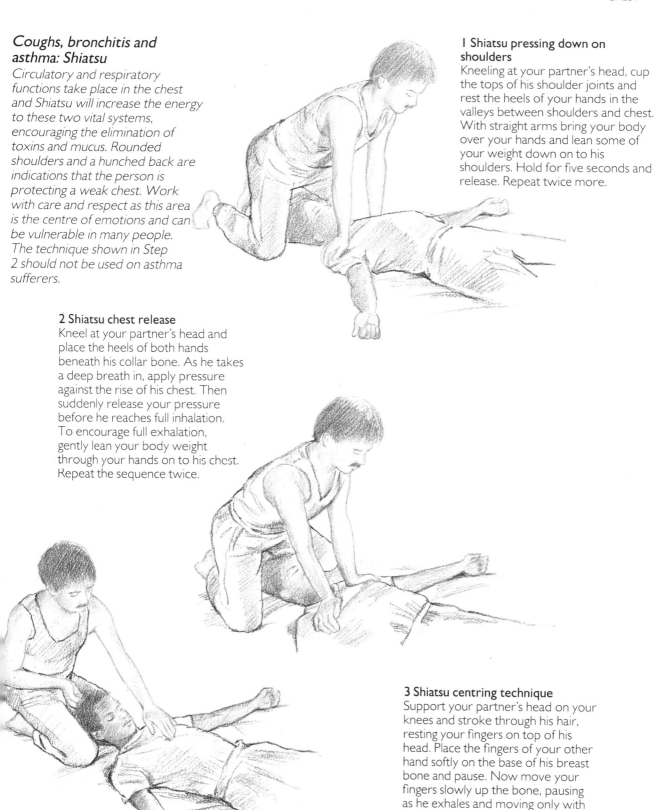

I Shiatsu pressing down on shoulders

Kneeling at your partner's head, cup the tops of his shoulder joints and rest the heels of your hands in the valleys between shoulders and chest. With straight arms bring your body over your hands and lean some of your weight down on to his shoulders. Hold for five seconds and release. Repeat twice more.

2 Shiatsu chest release

Kneel at your partner's head and place the heels of both hands beneath his collar bone. As he takes a deep breath in, apply pressure against the rise of his chest. Then suddenly release your pressure before he reaches full inhalation. To encourage full exhalation, gently lean your body weight through your hands on to his chest. Repeat the sequence twice.

3 Shiatsu centring technique

Support your partner's head on your knees and stroke through his hair, resting your fingers on top of his head. Place the fingers of your other hand softly on the base of his breast bone and pause. Now move your fingers slowly up the bone, pausing as he exhales and moving only with his inhalation.

ARMS AND HANDS

Our arms are crucial for our survival and how we relate to the world. Ever since we stood upright during the process of evolution we have been able to use our arms for a whole variety of activities, aided especially by our "opposable" thumbs. These thumbs probably make our hands the most skilful biological organs to have evolved. Our arms and hands are also vehicles of self-expression. They relate to the Throat and Heart *chakras* (see p.12) and with them we are able to express a huge range of feelings – from reaching out tenderly in love and affection, to expressing hatred and rage by beating or hitting, to warding off danger. As the arms, wrists and hands are so mobile and are used constantly in everyday activities, the joints and muscles can be subject to sprains or strains if they are stressed or overstretched (see p.90). These injuries can respond well to massage in their recuperative stages. Tennis elbow is a common strain of the arm for which we have given a massage sequence here. Hands and arms can also sometimes suffer from cramps, and the joints from rheumatic complaints such as arthritis (see p.92). Careful working with massage around the joints of the hand can bring relief and comfort.

Tennis elbow, cramp, strains

Tennis elbow is a strain caused by overstretching the muscles and tendons of the forearm at the outer side of the elbow, and pain is felt when the person grips or bends the arm when lifting heavy things. This strain can also happen after overuse in such activities as sawing. This sequence can be particularly helpful after an initial rest period and ice treatment (see p.91). Wait for one to two days before massaging. The sequence can also be helpful for cramp (see also p.85) or aching arms. Use rosemary essence here (see p.21).

Caution: *Before treating arthritic or injured joints see pp.90-3.*

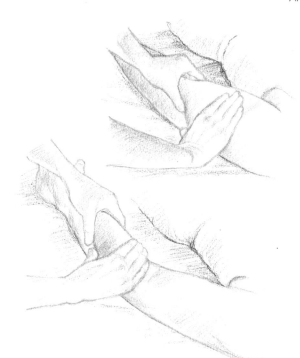

1 Kneading arms

With your partner lying down, face his side and begin to knead his upper arm with firm, rhythmical squeezing strokes. Travel right down to his wrist, giving special attention to the muscles of the forearm, just below the elbow. Knead thoroughly up and down the arm two or three times.

2 Massage around elbow joint

Support your partner's arm on your knee, so that his elbow is slightly raised. Now begin to work slowly with your thumbs and fingers around the whole joint, paying special attention to the outer (lateral) part of the elbow. Stay focused on the underlying structures, but if there is soreness, work with sensitivity.

3 Thumbing across fibres of forearm

Slightly raise your partner's lower arm and work first up the back, and then the front, of his forearm from the wrist with slow, firm thumb movements that push alternately upward and outward, crossing the fibres of the muscles that run down the arm. Give extra attention to the area just below the elbow.

Hand and wrist problems

Arthritic hands can benefit from gentle and sensitive massage around the joints. The sequence on these two pages may be useful and your partner can either lie or sit. Writer's cramp is muscle fatigue arising from any sustained, repetitive movement of the hand. Try out the strokes shown here, along with the hand massages from Whole Body (see p.40), to see which feel best. Fingers and thumbs can suffer from sprains or strains (see p.90) and massage can help healing and mobility in the recovery period.

Caution: *Before treating arthritic or injured joints see pp.90-3.*

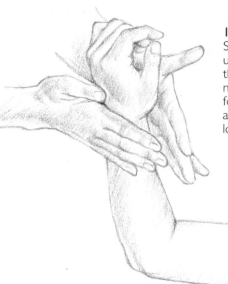

1 Wrist rolling

Support your partner's forearm in an upright position, with your palms on the back and front of his wrist. Now move your hands rapidly back and forth, rolling his wrist between them as you go. His hand should flop loosely as you do this stroke.

2 Flexing wrist

With his arm still upright, next stretch the back of the wrist. Support his hand by holding his wrist. With your free hand press down with your palm on the back of his hand. Do this slowly and carefully as you can reach the point of resistance quite quickly.

4 Opening the palm

Let your partner's palm face the floor and place the heels of your hands on the back of his hand and your fingers in his palm. Now press down with the heels of your hands and firmly lift with your fingers so that you open and spread the bones of his palm.

3 Extending wrist

With his arm in the same position, now stretch the front of his wrist by pushing down on his palm with your own palm. Press slowly to the point of resistance, then release. While you are doing this support his lower arm with your other hand.

5 Squeezing along channels

Holding your partner's hand in one hand, use the thumb and first finger of your other hand to squeeze along the channels between the bones. Press in firmly from both sides and work slowly along the groove from wrist to web of finger. It is easier to work two channels with one hand and two with the other.

6 Extending fingers

Stretch the inside of his knuckle joints by pressing your thumb on the back of his knuckle, with your other hand pushing the fingertip slowly backward till you reach the point of resistance. Ask your partner to say "when". Extend each finger in turn.

8 Stretching fingers

Begin, as before, by clasping the whole of your partner's finger, but this time begin to squeeze, wring, and stretch down the whole length of the finger to the tip and off, as shown below. Give firmest pressure on the root and especially along the ligaments at the sides of the finger.

7 Circling knuckle joint

Holding your partner's hand with one hand, clasp and isolate one of your partner's fingers by wrapping all the fingers of your other hand firmly around it, as shown above. Use your thumb to slowly circle around the knuckle joint, pushing into the softer tissue. Work each knuckle in this way, including the thumb.

STOMACH AND BELLY

The stomach and belly are a soft, sensitive, muscle-covered area of the body, unprotected by encircling bones (though the lower abdomen is in part protected by the bowl of the pelvis). Long ago, when we first became upright, we exposed our tender bellies to the world. This made us more vulnerable, but also able to relate more sensitively to one another. The stomach is also linked to the Solar Plexus *chakra* (see p.12), which is the seat of raw emotional energy, often of fear, but also of change and transmutation. Also on this level is the diaphragm, which separates chest from abdomen. Our breathing pattern is a vital gauge of our physical and emotional health. Stomach problems, such as indigestion, are often linked to anxiety and emotional causes; a surge of adrenalin can provoke a sudden sick feeling in the stomach. The belly houses the gut and also our "gut feelings". The *Hara chakra*, just below the navel, is our centre of gravity, strength and vitality. This is the centre from which we "ground" ourselves through our legs (see p.19). It is also closely linked with our sexuality. Tension and congestion here may cause constipation, flatulence or menstrual pain. Both massage and Shiatsu can help to ease complaints in the abdominal area.

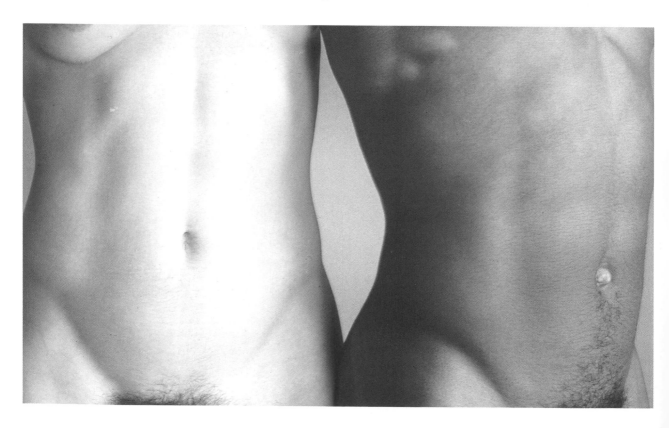

Indigestion and nausea

Indigestion can be the result of acid over-production due to stress, or eating too much, or foods that don't agree with us. The following strokes and techniques can help to soothe the discomfort. The vulnerable stomach must be worked on slowly, with great sensitivity. Camomile or cardamom essences (see p.21) can be helpful. Step 5 works by increasing the energy flow by linking the stomach with the stomach meridian. Step 6 is specifically for nausea and releases tightness in the area caused by stress.

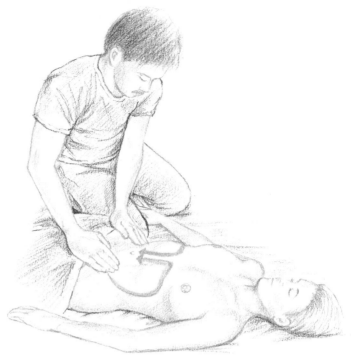

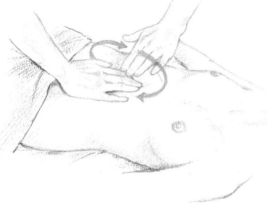

2 Gentle stroking down from ribs
Start at one side of your partner's ribcage and begin to glide your hands smoothly downward, one after the other. Move over the lower ribs, the base of the ribs, and on to the abdomen, with very light, slow strokes. Work right across the lower ribcage and repeat several times.

1 Light circling on sides and stomach
Kneel beside your partner's hip, facing her head, and rest your hands gently just inside her two hip bones. Now very lightly stroke up the sides of her torso, then across the lower ribs under her breasts. Stroke especially lightly down the centre, ending at the hip bones. Repeat the circling several times.

3 Holding stomach and circling back
With your partner lying on one side kneel by her back and rest one hand on her stomach just below her breast bone. With your other hand circle the mid back opposite your holding hand, in a counterclockwise direction. As you circle, relax your hand and stay present. Move your hand slowly, flowing over the forms.

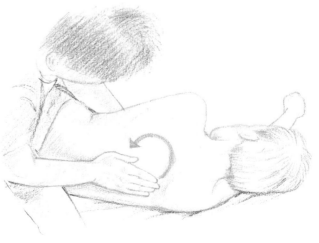

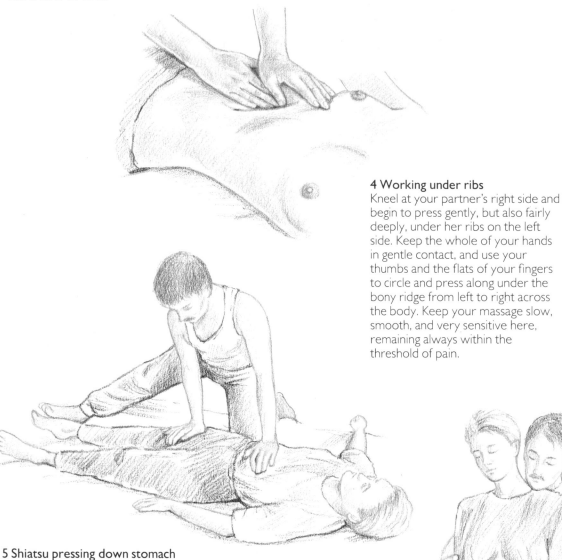

4 Working under ribs
Kneel at your partner's right side and begin to press gently, but also fairly deeply, under her ribs on the left side. Keep the whole of your hands in gentle contact, and use your thumbs and the flats of your fingers to circle and press along under the bony ridge from left to right across the body. Keep your massage slow, smooth, and very sensitive here, remaining always within the threshold of pain.

5 Shiatsu pressing down stomach meridian
Kneel by your partner and turn her leg inward by holding her foot with your foot. With your "mother hand" placed over the stomach area above the navel, palm down the front of her thigh with your active hand by leaning in with your body weight. Move slowly and repeat three times.

6 Shiatsu stroking along base of ribs
With your partner standing up stand behind her and bring your arms around her sides, letting your fingertips meet at the solar plexus. Now very lightly sweep both hands slowly out and away below the ribs and off the sides of the body. Repeat the technique several times.

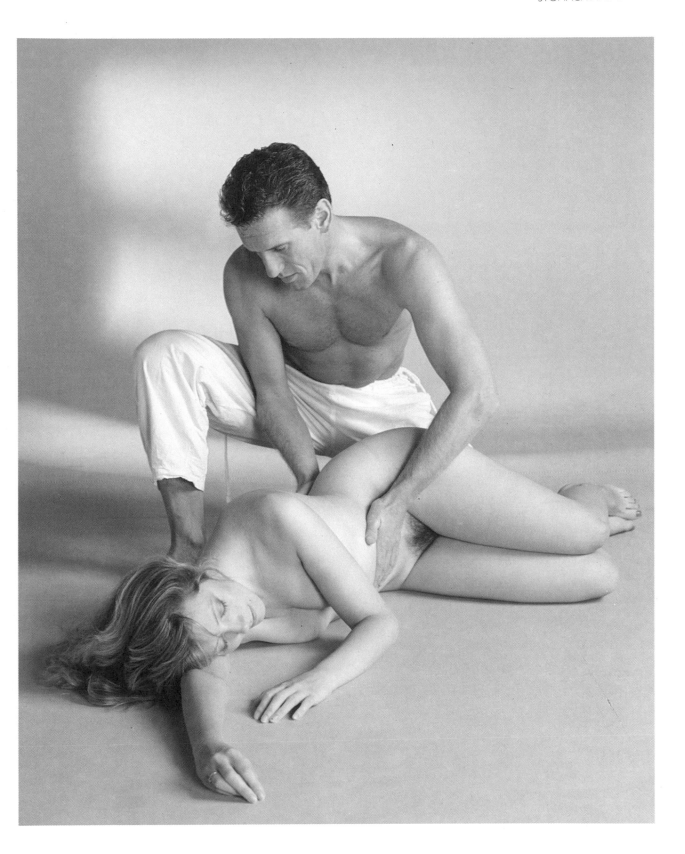

Constipation and flatulence

Constipation can be caused by lack of fibre in the diet, by emotional factors or by an inadequate fluid intake. Flatulence is a buildup of gases resulting in distention and discomfort. The first stroke (Step 1) works specifically with the colon and follows the direction of its wavelike muscular movements, which help to pass digested food along inside in a clockwise direction. With all these strokes on the belly area you should start lightly and gradually work in more deeply, with care and sensitivity. Always move slowly and stay aware of what your hands are sensing. Marjoram or fennel essences are suggested (see p.21).

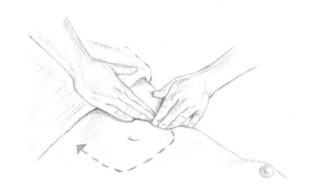

1 Working around colon
Kneel at your partner's right side and rest both your hands on the right of her lower abdomen. Start to work slowly upward with small firm circling strokes. Follow the direction of the colon, up to the right lower ribs, across to the left and then down to the inside of the left hip bone. Slide lightly across to the right side again and repeat.

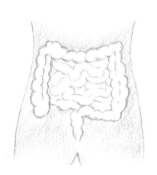

2 Pulling up sides
Reach across to your partner's far side and begin to pull up the side with slow generous strokes, your hands alternating and overlapping as they cover the area between ribs and hips. The movement should slightly lift and rock your partner. Let the stroke come from your pelvis. Repeat on the other side.

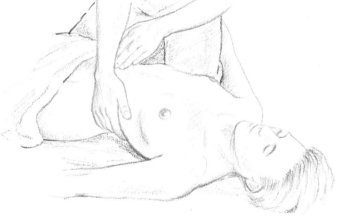

3 "Wave kneading" of belly
Lightly rest your hands on the centre of your partner's belly, one on top of the other. Using the heels of your hands push away across the belly and then let your hands curve over like a wave, so that your fingers come into contact and begin to pull back toward you. Continue to rock slowly back and forth rhythmically in this way for a short time.

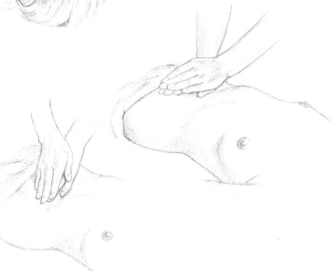

Menstrual pain

Painful periods usually result from hormonal imbalances in the body, and you might find it helpful to use some of these techniques to relieve tension in the area. Begin with slow circling on the sacrum, as this is very soothing. The sacral bone contains several pairs of holes from which nerves issue, and pressing these will help to relieve congestion. Rocking the pelvis relaxes the whole body and loosens the pelvic area. Massaging the legs can also help to relieve menstrual pain. Try using either camomile or jasmine essence (see p.21) for this problem.

Caution: *Seek medical advice if menstrual pain is persistent and/or severe.*

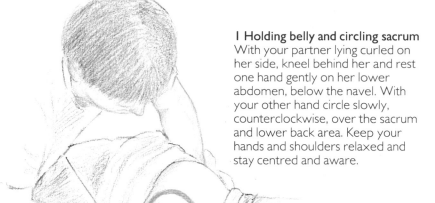

I Holding belly and circling sacrum

With your partner lying curled on her side, kneel behind her and rest one hand gently on her lower abdomen, below the navel. With your other hand circle slowly, counterclockwise, over the sacrum and lower back area. Keep your hands and shoulders relaxed and stay centred and aware.

2 Pressing into sacrum

With your partner lying on her front, kneel on one side of her thighs and place your thumbs at the top of her sacrum, keeping your fingers in contact with the body. Locate the two upper indentations and, coming forward from your *hara*, lean in with your thumbs. Hold for a moment and move on down the sacrum to the base, pressing in the same way.

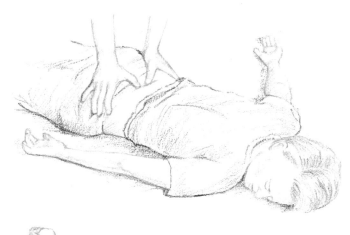

3 Rocking pelvis

Ask your partner to lie on her back and stand with one foot either side of her legs. Bend your knees and drop forward from your *hara*. Using your palms, start to rock her hips rhythmically from side to side. Once you have found a comfortable rhythm the rocking motion needs only a light touch to maintain it.

73

MID AND LOWER BACK

The back is the strength area of the body. Yet despite its strength more people have a back problem at some time in their lives than any other ailment. Lack of regular exercise, poor posture, tension and stress all contribute to our backs' proneness to aches and strains, and sometimes to more serious problems. One of these, the "slipped disc" occurs when the pad of cartilage between two vertebrae ruptures and some of the gel-like nucleus protrudes and presses against a nerve. Yet this is not always the cause of back pain. The large muscles of the back can suffer from strains that massage can often ease. The mid-back area relates to the Solar Plexus *chakra*, which is linked with emotion and change, and the lower back connects with both the *Hara* (strength, vitality and sexuality) and the Root *chakra* (our work, grounding and basic life situation – see p.12). Many back problems, and particularly those located in the lower back area, seem to have emotional causes, often linked to energy blocks and withheld mobility in the pelvic area. Since it is so vital to your back's health to have sufficient flexibility in the joints and muscles, we have included exercises to help your back to regain or retain its suppleness.

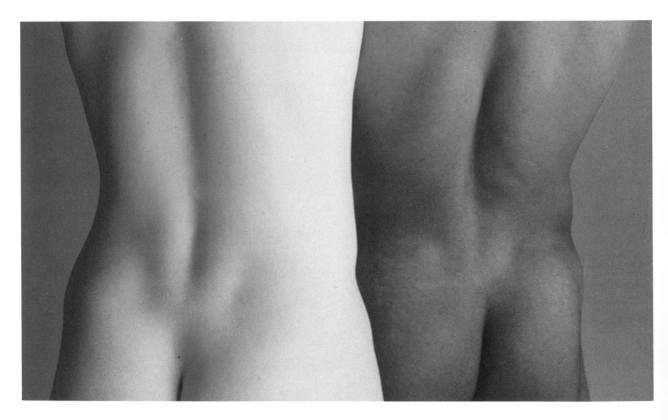

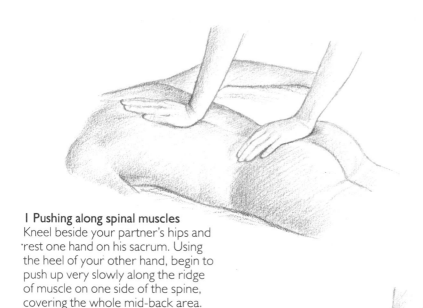

Mid backache

Aching in the mid back is often caused by tightness in the vertical bands of muscle on either side of the spine. Begin with slow gliding strokes and then move on to Steps 1 and 2, which work directly on the spinal muscles, Step 1 pushes up along the grain of the muscle and Step 2 works out across the fibres with the heels of your hands. Step 3 is performed with the soft inner parts of your forearms, and stretches the whole area with broad comforting movements. Try marjoram essence here (see p.21).

1 Pushing along spinal muscles

Kneel beside your partner's hips and rest one hand on his sacrum. Using the heel of your other hand, begin to push up very slowly along the ridge of muscle on one side of the spine, covering the whole mid-back area. Repeat several times along both sides of the spine, using your body weight to push up along the muscles.

2 Pushing across spinal muscles

Kneeling at your partner's side, knees apart, rest the heels of both your hands on the muscles at the far side of his spine, just below his shoulder blades. Lifting your hips up and forward, use some of your weight to push slowly out across the ridge of muscle. Move down the mid back in this way, then change sides and repeat the stroke.

3 Forearm stretch

Kneeling by your partner, rest the insides of your forearms on his mid back. Then glide them apart, one to the top of the neck and the other to the bottom of the sacrum. Start again at the mid back, but now glide your arms apart diagonally, so that one goes over one shoulder, the other over the opposite buttock. Repeat the stroke over the other buttock and shoulder.

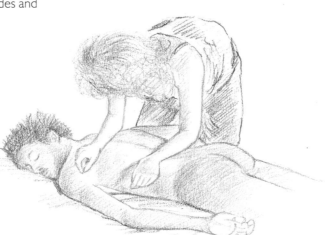

Lower backache

Lower back pain is one of the commonest of all the ailments treated in this book. As well as these massage strokes, which can be done in combination with lumbar circling (see Step 2, p.34), we show some useful stretching techniques. In Step 3 the receiver curls up in the yoga "child's pose" – if this is not comfortable you can achieve a similar effect by pressing down on your partner's knees (see Step 2, opposite page). Try rosemary essence (see p.21) for pain in this area.

Caution: *If back pain is severe and acute or if there are any other medical symptoms, consult a doctor, osteopath or chiropractor.*

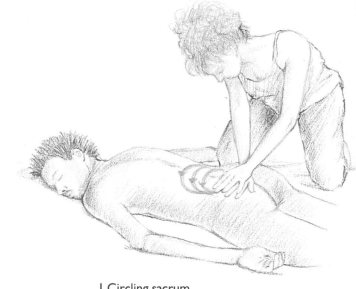

1 Circling sacrum

Kneel by your partner and rest both hands, one on top of the other, on his sacrum, as shown above. Now, transferring some of your weight forward on to your hands, start slow counterclockwise circles on the sacrum. Gradually extend them upward on to his lower back area, returning each time to the sacrum. Check how much pressure your partner prefers.

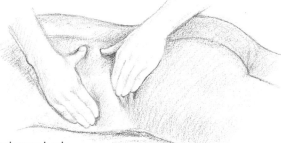

2 Kneading lower back

Now, using large, rhythmical rocking movements, knead the whole of your partner's lower back area on the opposite side, from work surface to spine. Use generous grasping and squeezing movements, with the whole of your hands, to work into the muscles slowly and thoroughly. Repeat on the other side.

3 "Child's pose" and back stretch

Ask your partner to kneel down with his forehead on the floor in the yoga "child's pose". If this is difficult, place a cushion between his buttocks and heels. Kneel by his side and rest one hand on the upper spine and the other on the base. Now press down so your hands push in opposite directions, stretching the spine.

1 Shiatsu back swing

With your partner lying on his back, stand astride his legs and raise his knees. Your feet should be shoulder-width apart and your knees bent. Now, using your forearms, lift his lower legs below the knees, resting your elbows on your own bent knees. Feel yourself firmly rooted on both legs, and sit back slowly on to your partner's feet. This will lift his pelvis an inch or two off the floor. Now swing his whole lower body gently from side to side.

Lower backache: Shiatsu

Shiatsu of the lower back aims to relax distorted muscles and so allow realignment of vertebrae. Pain in the lumbar area can be the effect of imbalance in the functioning of the kidneys, small intestines and the organs in the pelvis. Tight hamstrings also put extra stress on lower back muscles and techniques that stretch and loosen the back and legs as well as strengthening the hara will be beneficial. The lower back is an area that is weak in many people, so work slowly, with care, synchronizing your breath with your partner's and with your own movements, exhaling as you apply pressure.

2 Shiatsu pressing knees to chest

Begin as above, but this time rest your hands on the fronts of both your partner's knees, keeping your own knees bent and your shoulders relaxed. Use some of your weight to lean gently down, pressing his knees slowly toward his chest. Do not force past the point of resistance. Hold for a moment or two then release slowly.

3 Shiatsu holding *hara* and lower back

Kneeling beside your partner, slide one hand beneath his lower back, palm upward, and rest the other on his lower abdomen, or *hara*, just below the navel. Relax and tune in to your partner's breath. Imagine your hands are channels for healing energy that flows effortlessly through them. Hold for up to three minutes.

Sciatica

Sciatica is a sharp shooting pain felt in the legs and/or buttocks and back (usually on one side only), sometimes accompanied by a tingling in the corresponding leg or foot. It is caused when a disc bulges out between the vertebrae and presses against the sciatic nerve. Most disc protrusions heal themselves, given enough time and rest, and some of the strokes shown here may help to assist the healing process. Try the different movements and focus on those that afford most relief. Work slowly and be guided by your partner for the amount of pressure to use. Camomile or lavender essences (see p.21) may be helpful.

Caution: *If sciatic pain is persistent and severe and/or on both sides seek help from your doctor or an osteopath.*

1 Stretching to sides of sacrum
With your partner lying face down kneel by one thigh, facing his head. Place the heels of both your hands on his sacrum, with your fingers pointing outward. Now raise your pelvis and lean slowly forward on to your hands. Then gradually slide your hands away from his sacrum, out across the sides of his buttocks and off. Return to the sacrum and repeat a few times.

2 Kneading buttocks
Facing your partner's side at hip level, reach over to his opposite buttock and start to knead it with slow, firm circling movements, as shown above, using your whole hand. Focus with your fingers and thumbs, searching into the soft tissue between bones. Avoid areas of sharp pain – work around them, not directly on them, and always stay within the threshold of pain. Move around and repeat on the other side.

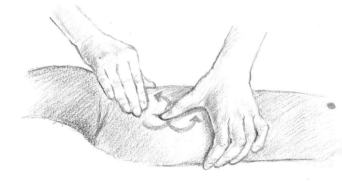

3 Circling down back of leg
With the fingers of one hand and the thumb of the other, trace small overlapping circles down the back of one thigh. Ease the pressure at the back of the knee, then pause to press gently on the Shiatsu *tsubo* (marked) with your thumb. Then continue to circle down to the lower calf. Repeat on the other leg.

4 Heel-of-hand pressure on buttocks

Facing toward your partner's head, place the heels of both your hands on the hollows at the sides of his buttocks, as shown left. Slowly press your hands in toward each other. Try gently rocking the pelvis from side to side, or use alternating or synchronized circling movements to work into the soft tissue. Go gently if there is any tenderness.

5 Pressing sacrum holes and under iliac crests

Kneeling by your partner's thigh, facing his head, rest your thumbs on either side of the top of his sacrum. Feel for the small hollows, then slowly lean on to your thumbs. Hold, release, then move down the sacrum, pressing the pairs of holes. Now press carefully outward along under the rims of the pelvic bone, as shown right.

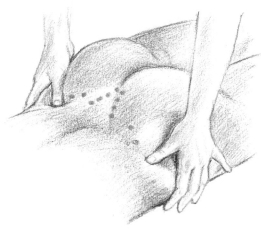

6 Stretching legs

Kneel at your partner's feet and take hold of one foot, one hand cupped around his heel and the other supporting the front of his ankle joint. Now lean back from your pelvis and let your arms go taut like ropes. Let your body take the weight and stretch the leg steadily and firmly. Release, then repeat on the other foot.

Aching hips

The hips act as the body's fulcrum, joining legs with torso. Many people hold tension here, due to lack of exercise, structural imbalance in the legs and suppression of sexuality and anger (both basic drives centred in the hara). This creates stagnation in the pelvis and increasingly limited and painful movement of the hip joints. Pressing in the buttocks around the hip joints and rotating them by moving the legs will increase circulation and mobility and help to relieve discomfort. The whole of the sequence for sciatica (see pp.78-9) will also be useful for warming and loosening the muscles around the hip joint. Try marjoram essence for massaging hips (see p.21).

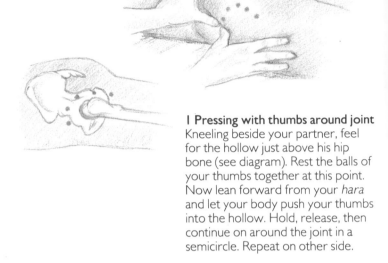

1 Pressing with thumbs around joint
Kneeling beside your partner, feel for the hollow just above his hip bone (see diagram). Rest the balls of your thumbs together at this point. Now lean forward from your *hara* and let your body push your thumbs into the hollow. Hold, release, then continue on around the joint in a semicircle. Repeat on other side.

2 Shiatsu rotating hip joint
With your partner on his back, kneel on one knee by his thigh, facing his head. Raise his leg, as shown left, using one hand on his knee and the other on his ankle. Start slowly to rotate the hip joint by describing small circles with his knee. Gradually extend the circles to the point of resistance, then reverse the direction of rotation. Repeat on the other hip.

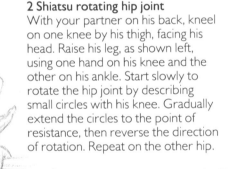

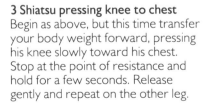

3 Shiatsu pressing knee to chest
Begin as above, but this time transfer your body weight forward, pressing his knee slowly toward his chest. Stop at the point of resistance and hold for a few seconds. Release gently and repeat on the other leg.

1 Breathing into pain

Lie on your back with your knees up, feet hip-width apart, and your arms and shoulders relaxed. Locate an area of pain or tension in your body, and as you inhale, imagine your breath bringing healing energy and nourishment to this area. As you exhale imagine breathing out the tension or soreness with your breath. Breathe slowly and deeply in this way for several minutes.

Exercises for mid or lower back pain

If we kept our backs healthy and supple with regular exercise and if we were aware of our posture, many back problems would be avoided. Here is a series of exercises to do daily. Never overstrain when exercising and move smoothly and slowly. Do each exercise only for as long as feels comfortable. Breathing properly (i.e. inhaling as you spread out your body and exhaling as you curl in) will aid circulation and help to heal strained muscles. Work up gradually to the half sit-ups and take pain as a warning to go more easily. A pillow under the pelvis may help to ease the lower back.

2 Pelvic lift

Lying as before, with your feet flat on the floor, lift the base of your spine and pelvis slightly by tightening the muscles of your abdomen and squeezing your buttocks together. As you do this, make sure your neck and shoulders remain relaxed. Hold for a count of five and then relax all the muscles and begin again. Repeat.

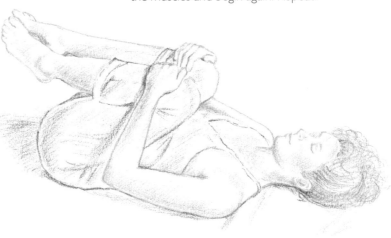

3 Bringing knees to chest

Lie on your back with your knees up, and hold them with your hands. As you exhale, bring them gradually toward your chest to the point of resistance. You can bounce them very slightly in this position if it feels comfortable. As you inhale, gently lower them again until your feet touch the floor. Repeat.

4 Letting one knee fall out to side
Lie on your back as before, with your knees up and feet apart. As you inhale, let one of your knees flop out to the side. Keep your neck and shoulders relaxed. Lift your leg again as you exhale and on the next inhalation let your other leg flop out to the other side. Repeat.

5 Gentle twist
Start as before and, as you inhale, let both your knees flop to one side so that your pelvis rolls from the hips. Keep your shoulders on the floor as you do this and for extra twist gently roll your head to the opposite side. As you exhale, bring your knees back up to centre again and, on the next inhalation, let your pelvis roll to the other side. Repeat.

6 Partial sit-ups
Lying on your back with your knees slightly bent, gently raise your neck and upper back off the floor as you exhale, stretching your arms forward at the same time. Hold for a count of five and then very slowly uncurl backward so that your back, then your neck, your head, and finally your arms are relaxing again on the floor. Repeat.

LEGS AND FEET

Our legs and feet support us, transport us, and connect us with the ground beneath. They link with our sense of security and stability – or lack of it. Many expressions in our language reflect the legs' connection with security: "to stand on our own two feet"; "to stand our ground"; "to be a person of standing" and "having our feet firmly on the ground". Locking our knees and bracing our legs can give us a false sense of security, but in fact this increases our susceptibility to shock or injury as it makes our joints less flexible. The legs link with the *hara* (our centre of gravity) and the Root *chakra* (our grounding and root situation in life, see p.12). The Root *chakra* is at the base of the spine and it is from here that the nerves emerge to supply the legs and feet, which are indeed our "mobile roots". Our feet are complex structures, each having 26 bones and an arch, which have to support the weight of the whole body above, and act as shock absorbers. Massage brings awareness to our legs and feet, helps to improve our circulation, clears waste and toxins and generally increases our sense of connection with the ground.

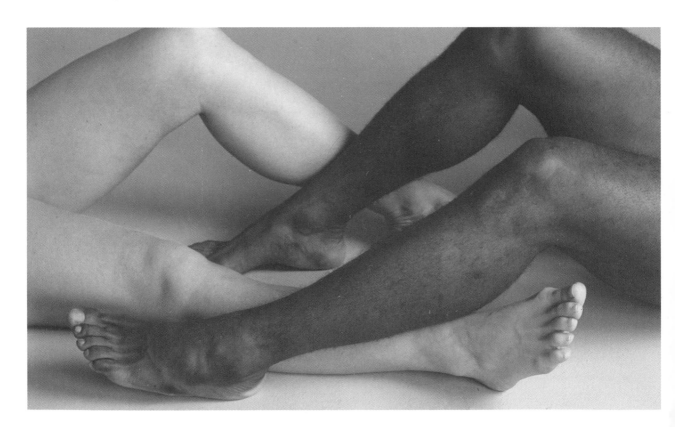

Cramp

Cramp is a painful, sharp and sudden contraction of muscles. It occurs most frequently in the legs or feet, but can happen in other parts of the body as well. Cramp is sometimes caused by salt loss after very excessive sweating, or by poor circulation. It can be violent and come on suddenly in the night. In this sequence we show some alternating kneading and stretching movements for the calf muscle. As well as massaging the leg it is often helpful to get up and walk about in order to stretch the tightening muscles. Marjoram essence may be helpful (see p.21).

1 Stretching back of leg

Kneel at your partner's foot and, cupping one hand under his heel, lift his leg slowly to stretch the muscles at the back of the leg. To emphasize the stretch you can use your other hand to press his foot back toward his head. Hold the stretch for a few seconds, then release. Then repeat as many times as are necessary.

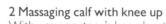

2 Massaging calf with knee up

With your partner's knee bent, kneel on either side of his foot and begin to work, with both hands, into his calf muscle using slow, rhythmical kneading and wringing strokes. Squeeze, press and lift the muscles, using one hand after the other. You can alternate this muscle massage with stretches of the back of his leg, as shown in Step 1.

3 Kneading the calf

With your partner lying on his front, kneel at his side and begin firmly to knead the calf muscle. Rock your body from your pelvis as you lift, circle, and squeeze with alternate hands. Cover the whole calf area thoroughly.

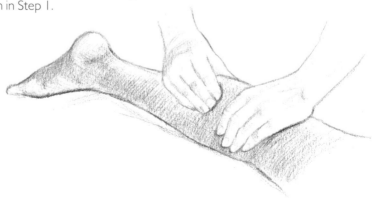

Knee ache, arthritis, sprains and strains

As they are large weight-bearing joints, the knees are subject to powerful forces, making them susceptible to physical stress. This happens particularly if they are usually held braced or locked. The massage sequence shown here will help the healing process after any structural damage from injury has been repaired (see p.90). The strokes will also ease tired, aching knee joints and help arthritic knees (see p.92). The receiver can sit in a chair, if lying on the floor is not comfortable. Try using lavender or rosemary essence (see p.21).

Caution: If the joint is inflamed or swollen, do not massage it, but work the muscles above and away from the swelling to disperse fluid.

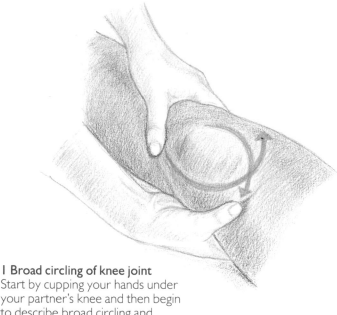

1 Broad circling of knee joint

Start by cupping your hands under your partner's knee and then begin to describe broad circling and overlapping movements right around the front of his knee with your thumbs. Move rhythmically in alternating circles. As your thumbs work over the front of his knee joint your fingers and palms are sliding under and massaging both the sides and the back of the joint.

2 Deep tissue work

Kneeling between or beside your partner's legs, start to work slowly and sensitively around the knee using both your fingers and thumbs to press into the soft tissue between the bones. You can use small rotating movements, without sliding on the skin, as you press in. Stay present and work right around the knee, keeping within the threshold of pain.

3 Massaging muscles above knee

Rest your hands on either side of your partner's leg, just above his knee, and use your thumbs to make slow, firm sweeping movements, upward and outward, over the muscles above the knee. Pay special attention to this area and then work gradually up the front of the thigh in the same way.

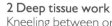

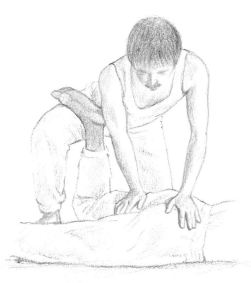

1 Shiatsu palming down back of thigh

With your partner lying on his front, kneel on one knee and support his bent leg on your other knee. Rest one hand on his sacrum and, with your other hand, palm slowly down the back of his thigh. Build up and release each pressure by moving your body weight on to and off your active hand. Repeat on the other leg.

2 Shiatsu kneeling on feet and pressing calves

Carefully kneel on the soles of your partner's feet and place the palms of your hands on his calves. Increase your pressure by slowly moving your body weight on to your knees and hands, and begin to massage his calves. You can also work on your partner's thighs from this position.

Leg ache: Shiatsu

Energy can easily stagnate and toxins can build up in the feet and legs due to lack of exercise and movement. This causes the circulation of blood returning to the heart to become sluggish under the pull of gravity. Many major meridians and nerves run to and from the feet and legs, connecting them to vital organs and glands, and when a buildup of impurities continues the legs ache and the whole of the body is adversely affected. Pressing down on the legs and walking on the receiver's feet activates the movement of energy and encourages the dispersal of toxins.

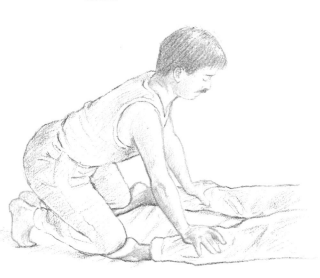

3 Shiatsu treading on feet

For this technique, your partner's feet should lie flat, with the heels falling out to the sides. Using your heels, walk on the soles of his feet. Put pressure only on the insteps and balls of his feet, and take care not to step on his heels. If there is space between his ankles and the floor, insert a rolled towel to fill the gap.

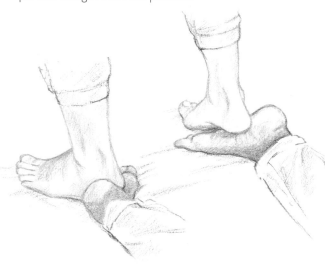

Footache, sprains and strains, arthritis

Foot massage is wonderfully refreshing and relaxing and, because of the hundreds of nerve endings on the sole of the foot that have reflex connections with all parts of the body, it can relax the whole body as well. The sequence here can be used in combination with the foot strokes shown for the whole body (see p.36), and will help in the recovery stage of strains or sprains (see p.90). Try rosemary or bergamot essences (see p.21).

Caution: *Do not massage swollen or inflamed joints. Before treating arthritis see p.92.*

1 Rotating ankle joint
With your partner lying on his front, lift his lower leg. Now clasp the side of the big toe joint and let your inner forearm rest on his heel. Using your forearm like a lever rotate the whole foot in a slow, wide circle, first in one direction and then in the other.

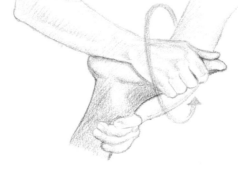

2 Pushing front of foot back
Kneel beside your partner and with one hand press down on his heel and use the other to push the front of his foot back toward his head. Press to the point of resistance, then hold, and release.

3 Pressing down on ball of foot
Kneel up, and with one hand, hold either side of the Achilles tendon, just below your partner's heel. With your other hand, press down on the ball of his foot (not on the toes alone), while pushing the heel up. Lean firmly in to this stretch, but check the limit with your partner.

4 Twisting front of foot to sides
Still kneeling, face down toward your partner's toes. Clasp each side of the front of his foot. Now slowly twist it sideways, first to one side and then the other. Repeat several times.

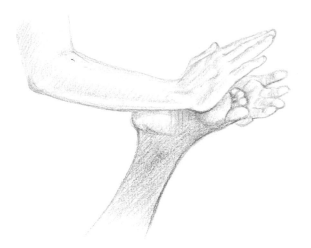

5 Rolling ball of foot between heels of hands

Sandwich the ball of your partner's foot (back and front) between the heels of your hands. Now roll the ball of his foot between them and, with a firm rotating pressure, move from side to side, covering the whole of the area just behind the toes.

6 Stretching toes apart

Hold two adjacent toes between the thumbs and fingers of your hands and slowly pull them apart from each other, stretching the web of skin. Let your partner tell you when the stretch is enough. Stretch all the toes in this way.

7 Pulling toes

Facing up toward your partner's head, hold his foot with one hand. With your other hand, take hold of a toe between your thumb and finger and gently but firmly rotate it a few times. Then stretch it with a steady pull before sliding your fingers to the tip and off. Repeat on every toe.

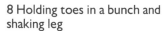

8 Holding toes in a bunch and shaking leg

Face toward your partner's head and, with one hand, grasp his toes in a bunch between the heel of your hand and the flats of your fingers (avoid "clawing" in under the toes). With your other hand, take hold of the big toe and joint and then with both hands, lift the leg slightly and shake it a little, thereby stretching all the toes at once. Repeat from Step 1 on the other foot.

Sprains and strains

A strain is an injury to muscle fibres or ligaments that have been forcibly stretched beyond their proper length. This can result in some local pain and perhaps swelling. A sprain is more severe and is caused by a violent wrench or twist, causing tearing of the muscle fibres or the ligaments of a joint, resulting in pain, swelling and bruising. The most common areas to be affected are wrists, ankles and backs. These are both common injuries that can be helped by massage in the recovery stages, but you will need to follow the process outlined below. Having ascertained from a doctor that no bones are broken, the best initial treatment for sprains and strains is an ice pack or a cold-water compress if no ice is available. Then you should apply a bandage and support the joint, elevating it if possible. Rest for between 24 and 48 hours, or until tenderness has subsided. Remedial massage treatment can then begin.

Don't work directly on swollen areas, but start with gentle gliding strokes that push up toward the heart, above the injury. In the case of a sprained ankle, for example, work first from knee to thigh, and then from ankle to knee, to help disperse the fluid (see below). As the injury heals you can begin to work all around the area with careful kneading and friction strokes. Finally, where possible, you can work with passive movements to help restore mobility. Always keep within the threshold of pain. You could use a mixture of lavender and rosemary essences (see p.21).

Draining above swelling in sprained ankle

With your partner lying down, his knee supported with a cushion, begin to stroke slowly upward, first on the thigh from knee to top of leg. After several minutes do the same on the lower leg, working above the ankle and up toward the knee. Use alternating hand movements, gently squeezing and pushing in the direction of the heart to aid the dispersal of fluid from the joint along the blood and lymph vessels.

Ice and water compresses

For sprains and strains ice is useful for reducing internal bleeding, but you should never apply ice directly to the skin. Always wrap it in a cloth, or use a bag of frozen peas. Apply ice for five minutes in every hour, for several hours, during the first day or two. If you do not have any ice, a cloth wrung out in cold water is also effective. Where there is persistent aching from strained muscles, alternating hot and cold compresses can bring relief.

Applying hot and cold compresses

You need two bowls, one containing iced water and the other very hot (not boiling) water, and two cotton cloths or small towels. It is useful to start with the hot compress, so wring out one cloth in the hot water, then fold it to shape and apply it to the area of pain for three minutes. Next wring out the cold cloth and apply it for one minute. Continue alternating these compresses for between ten and fifteen minutes.

Arthritis

There are many different kinds of arthritis, all of them involving the joints. The most common are rheumatoid arthritis and osteoarthritis. Rheumatoid arthritis is a generalized disease that can start in childhood, usually in the small bones of the hands or feet. Joints become very painful, swollen and inflamed, and the condition can spread throughout the body. Osteoarthritis is a disease of later life, linked with wear and tear and mechanical deterioration of joints, bones and discs. It is often found first in the lower neck and lower back, and can occur in joints where there have been previous injuries. Massage can help to reduce pain in both these ailments. However, if a joint is swollen or inflamed do not work on it. You may give it hand healing by just resting your hands lightly on the painful area for several minutes while remaining centred. Then work with light gliding strokes above the swelling, in the direction of the heart. Where there is no swelling you can use whatever strokes feel good to your partner, from the section of the book that deals with that part of the body.

Before doing passive movements on arthritic joints check with a doctor to see if this is alright and then always go very sensitively and keep within the pain threshold. Never force movements beyond their range. General soothing, slow stroking and gentle kneading and thumb circling around the affected areas can be comforting and relaxing. Rosemary and lavender essences dissolved in oil will also help to alleviate pain (see p.21).

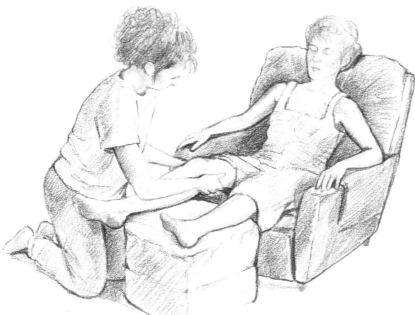

Supporting the limb
As people with arthritis may feel too stiff to climb on to a table or get down on to the floor you can improvise in a variety of ways with chairs of different kinds, and stools or footstools to support the legs. Watch your own posture and avoid bending too much. Sit on the floor or on a stool or chair as you work.

When massage should not be used

There are certain conditions which should not be treated by massage or Shiatsu and these are listed below. It is very important to take note of these contraindications. However, the fact that a person is suffering from any of these ailments does not mean that he or she should be totally deprived of any healing touch. Touch is reassuring, calming and comforting and can help to mobilize the body's own healing processes. So very gentle touching or light stroking on unaffected areas of the body can be soothing and help to ease pain. For any serious problem, though, never massage without first obtaining a doctor's consent. The warning "Don't massage" means don't use any deep strokes on or near the affected areas.

Hand healing
Hand healing is done by first centring (see p.19) and then very gently letting your hands come to rest on a part, or two parts, of the body and holding them lightly there for some minutes. Meanwhile you remain present and aware and visualize your hands as channels for healing energy.

Contraindications

Localized infections or inflammation
Don't: massage where there is an infection or inflammation, as you may spread it.
You may: do very light hand healing through clothes or dressings. With a doctor's consent do gentle stroking massage on parts of the body that are not sites of infection.

Swelling
Don't: massage on swollen areas.
You may: do light hand healing and work above swelling with upward strokes to disperse fluid.

Skin eruptions (i.e. acne, eczema, heat rash)
Don't: massage over skin eruptions.
You may: do light hand healing through clothes and massage on parts that are clear, draining upward to drain wastes from tissue.

Bruising
Don't: massage on bruises.
You may: work upward above the bruise and stroke around it to disperse it.

Varicose veins
Don't: massage on varicose veins, and don't push up from below toward them.
You may: do hand healing, apply cold-water compresses (see p.91), elevate the leg and do gentle gliding strokes above the varicose veins, up toward the heart. If a doctor agrees you can also work with very light, slow upward strokes on either side of the veins, not directly on them. This can relieve the aching caused by swollen varicose veins.

Fever
Don't: massage a person with a fever.
You may: do hand healing. The skin is often hypersensitive during a fever. Stroking or holding may give comfort.

Thrombosis or phlebitis
Don't: massage a person with these conditions, which mean that blood clots are present and massage could dislodge them.
You may: do light hand healing or do very gentle massage of hands, feet or face if a doctor agrees.

Broken bones
Don't: massage if a bone is broken or suspected to be broken. Seek medical help.
You may: give hand healing and comforting touch to other parts of the body for reassurance. In later healing stages consult a doctor, then massage as for sprains and strains.

Tumours
Don't: massage where there are tumours.
You may: do hand healing. If a doctor agrees do gentle stroking of areas such as face, feet, hands and shoulders. Cancer patients can get great comfort from caring touch.

Pregnancy
Don't: use Shiatsu pressure around ankles or massage with any heavy, deep or percussion strokes on lower back or abdominal areas.
You may: with the consent of a doctor, give gentle massage throughout pregnancy, using light and gentle strokes but be particularly careful in the first three months.

Publisher's acknowledgements
Gaia would like to extend special thanks to the following:
Sara Thomas, Jane Downer, Chris Jarmey, Sheilagh Noble,
Fausto Dorelli, Lesley Gilbert, Peter Sperryn, Sara
Mathews, all the photographic models, and the staff at
Marlin Graphics Ltd and F. E. Burman.

Author's acknowledgements
First of all I want to thank Chris Sturgess-Lief, who
encouraged me to write the book when it was still only an
idea. I also would like to thank Jane Downer for her
contribution on Shiatsu and her invaluable help and support
(and wonderful Shiatsu treatments). Thanks also to Chris
Jarmey for his advice. I want to thank Lucy Lidell for her
work on the book, and all her support and clarity. Many
thanks to Joanna Godfrey Wood for all her hard work,
co-operation and patience in editing, also to Susan
McKeever, and to Lynn Hector for her design and patience.
Thanks to Fausto Dorelli for his beautiful photographs and
to Sheilagh Noble for her sensitive drawings. Thanks, too,
to Peter Sperryn as my medical advisor, and to Mary-Jane
Anderton and Anita Sullivan. Gratitude also to those who
modelled for the photographs and drawings: Jane Downer,
Terry Williams, Karen Drury, Patti Money-Coutts, Jerry
Gloag, Otter Baker, Michael Tirrell, David Kayla-Joseph
and friend Mike, Danny Paradise and Margareeta Saari.
Finally, special thanks to Bob Moore for his healing and
inspiration.

Recommended reading

Brooks, Charles, *Sensory Awareness*, Viking Press, 1974

Downing, George, *The Massage Book*, Wildwood House,
1973

Lidell, Lucinda, *The Book of Massage*, Ebury Press, 1984

Masunaga, Shizuto, *Zen Shiatsu*, Japan Publications, 1977

Montague, Ashley, *Touching*, Harper and Row, 1971

Ohashi, Wataru, *Do-it-yourself Shiatsu*, Unwin Paperbacks,
1976

Tanner, John, *Beating Back Pain*, Dorling Kindersley, 1987

Von Durkheim, Eraf Karlfried, *Hara: the Vital Centre of
Man*, Unwin Paperbacks, 1977

Sources of quotes on p.7
Gunter, Bernard, *Massage*, Academy Editions, 1973

Liss, Jerome, *In the Wake of Reich*, Coventure Ltd, 1976

Brooks, Charles, *Sensory Awareness*, Viking Press, 1974

Useful addresses
Sara Thomas
15A Bridge Avenue
London W6 9JA

Jane Downer
92 Chesson Rd
London W14 9QU

Chris Jarmey
(Shiatsu School of Natural
Therapy)
Churchfield Cottage
East Kennet
Nr Marlborough
Wiltshire SN8 4EY
tel. 0672 86459